For Don,

My Life, my route is Christ. Indeed, it was a bit of a Rocky Road, but I found my way!

I asked God for help and He Answered.

Hope you feel better Soon.

Bob Schultz

(Bob The Elder)

January 2018

God's Blessings!

MW00889285

I

Coming of Age and More

Introduction
Written by R.A.Schultz

A.K.A. Robert, Bud, Bob, Dad, Pop, Stroker, Gramps, Grandpa, The Flycaster and a few others

This is a collection of short stories   about my Life and the people I Love. I have tried to keep it as factual as my memory would allow. Thanks to all that responded to my communications to help refresh my memory.

My **Coming of Age** begins at Niagara Falls, New York in a hospital that overlooks the actual water fall. As of this writing, my actual **Coming of Age** continues to evolve in Corpus Christi, Texas.

I am still uncertain if I have totally **Come of Age**. There is most certainly a very young boy running around inside this body desperately trying to get out for just a bit more mischief.

I hope that after reading my memoirs, your opinion of me has not been adversely affected.

My apologies to Mrs. Rosso, my high school English teacher. I did the best I could. If I have gone, you need to know that **I deeply loved all of you.**

Live a FULL life, take a ride around the 'Bankers Turn' !

- I dedicate this book to those I loved that have gone before me. Mom & Dad, my sister Margaret and friends, Paul, Tim, Eddie, Bummer, Kenny, Tom, Clyde, Roy, Rudy, Herb and my Dog Gus

Table of Contents

Coming of Age and More

Prologue

Coming of Age and More is in effect, the story of my life. I am omitting the sad stories with the hope that I can make you laugh or at least smile about funny, silly and yes dumb things I have seen and done. There are a couple of stories that are sad. I could find no way around them, because they were important chapters of my life.

I am compiling this book so those that come after me will know where I came from and where I hope I am going. This book is for my sons Jeffrey and Michael and my stepdaughter Britt, who became the daughter I love. My thanks to my beautiful proof reader, editor and wife Suzanne.

The story begins in the early 1940's at Niagara Falls, New York where I was born. In those days, you could actually see the water and Niagara Falls itself from the hospital where I was born.

My father was first generation American and my mother emigrated from England. Dad was a skilled Carpenter and in the 1920's played semi-pro baseball in Florida. My mother was a bookkeeper for the Cunningham Oldsmobile car dealership for many years.

During the Great Depression, my father became a rather well known golfer in the city because my mother had a job all through the depression years. Mom bought my dad season passes for the city golf courses and that kept him from going crazy... .suicide at that time was a daily thing in the city.

To beat the mental depression, my dad would walk every day to the factory where he'd been laid off to see if there was any 'Day' work. The answer was usually no, so he would walk another few miles to the golf course and play a minimum of 36 holes.

Then he would walk home following the New York Central railroad looking for pieces of coal that had fallen from the tender car behind the steam engines. The coal was a prize because it burned many times longer than wood in the stove we used for both cooking and heating. And this was repeated five days a week.

Because of this routine, my dad was very proficient with a golf club. When touring golf pro's came to the city for a match play competition, they did not bring their own caddie, so they would ask for a good golfer to caddie for them. My dad usually got the job.

He carried sticks for a lot of famous golfers that I remember. His favorite was Jimmy Demaret. Dad thought he was a truly nice man.

I was fortunate to be able to play a lot of golf with my dad. I think he was in his seventies when I finally beat him. The norm was I would boom a drive way over there and my dad would hit a drive of maybe 220 yards straight down the middle. He always laughed at me saying "It's not how far, it's where". At the end of the day the totals would say I had lost yet again. I cherish those days.

My Christian beliefs began with Dad. Every Sunday, I was expected to be in church seated next to him. In my whole life, I never heard my father say a profane word. Not ever. Admittedly, I was not a good Christian for a lot of years, but the seeds were planted so to speak. Later in life things happened in my life where I asked for Divine help, a wake up call if you will.

I lost my parents within four months of each other. Their ashes are mixed together and they share a common grave. I am happy that they are at rest together.

My sister Margaret (Peggy)

I was the second born in our family, the first was my sister Margaret. I lost her to leukemia when she was 38. She was the smart one, Valedictorian, all that stuff. My dad never really got over it and neither have I.

At the age of four, we moved to Ransomville and that is where the real story begins. The photo is of my Mom, Alice at the old farm house. It now has a historical marker on it.

VII

The Culp family

When my mother, Alice Howarth, was still an infant, her father died while they were still living in England. Grand mother, mom and her brother Frank, emigrated to the United States. Mom was only four years old. How scary that must have been.

Later in my life, doing some research, I found the death certificate for my maternal grandfather. It listed the cause of death as "Consumption". What? I had heard that term before but never knew what "Consumption" was. I think John Wayne died from "Consumption" in one of his movies.

Internet search, "Consumption, a gradual withering away of the body." Seems like a 'catch all phrase' for anything the medical community did not understand. T.B.? Cancer? M.S.? M.D.? Who knows?

Some time after entering the United States, My Grandmother met and married Elgin Culp. A distinguished gentleman who's family came to the United States in 1744 and settled in Gettysburg Pennsylvania. I think Elgin was either 5th or more likely 6th generation to be born in the United States.

Elgin

A couple notable items about grandpa Culp. He was a proper gentleman. I never saw him dressed in any fashion other than a three piece suit. Working in his garden, everywhere, a three piece suit was the attire of the day.

When grandpa died, I was very young, maybe six years old. He was putting on window screens for the summer. Grandma found him in the back yard, flat on his back, still holding a window screen and he was appropriately dressed for burial.

I never remember Grandpa saying one word, EVER! A true quiet man.

Grandpa Culp had a habit, that gave me many a nightmare. Their home in Niagara Falls, New York was called their cottage. It was pretty cool to me. Looking out the front windows was Whirlpool Avenue. On the other side of the street was railroad tracks. The best part was everything in view was Canada! You see, beyond the railroad was the Niagara river gorge about one mile downstream from the Niagara Falls itself. Walk across the rail tracks, look to the left, there in the distance was the water falls. Keep on walking West a very few steps and it would mean sudden death. The Niagara river gorge has verticle walls and the gorge is deep. When I was growing up, there were no fences. I do not even remember any warning signs either.

Today, there is a walking trail all along the gorge with a masonry wall that you would have to climb over in the event you wanted to impersonate Peter Pan.

I always wondered why so many people traveled thousands of miles to Niagara Falls then waded out in the river to be swept over the Falls to their death? I also wondered how many changed their minds half way through their fall? My Uncle found one of the 'Jumpers' washed up in front of his cabin. He had been missing for a week. Not pretty. That trip would be, over the falls, North on the Niagara river about 10 miles, then East in Lake Ontario about four miles to my Uncles' Cabin. EWW!

Sorry, the scary part about Grandpa Elgin. Their cottage had one of those big cast iron stoves in the kitchen that grandma cooked on every day. It was a wood burning stove. In that part of the country, coal was the fuel of choice. Because of the fuel, the stove was burning 24/7. No on off switches. That stove was HOT. I didn't have to be warned, I stayed well away.

Now here comes grandpa Culp, Every day, around 2 PM, it was time for a snooze. Not saying a word to anyone, he would walk up to the front of the stove, fold his hands behind his back, lean over the stove a bit and within seconds, he was sound asleep. STANDING ! ASLEEP ! OVER A RED HOT STOVE ! How horrifying to this kid. I just knew he was going to become "Old Griddle Face" at any time. Didn't happen. Amazing. I thought it was an act. Grandma said it was the same, every day.

The Culp Brothers?

When I was seven years old, our family made a vacation trip to Washington D.C. One of the stops was to tour Gettysburg, that was the home of many generations of the Culp family. I remember being in the Museum at the Battleground and my mom showing me a picture that was hanging of a Cavalry officer named Captain Culp. I was told he was a great, great cousin (by marriage) of mine. She explained that he fought for the Union and his brother, Wesley, a private, fought for the Confederacy. They met in battle at Gettysburg. Wesley was killed in battle. He was attempting to deliver a letter from the Captains girlfriend to his brother. This research proved to be wrong. Capt. Culp gave Wesley a letter for his girlfriend in Gettysburg, while being held as a prisoner.

Captain William Culp

87th Pennsylvania Regiment

Private Wesley Culp

2nd Virginia Regiment

In 2001 I took my wife to see if my memory was still okay. Sure enough, there in the museum was a really nice display about Captain William and Private Wesley. How cool.

But wait, I started doing some research and there were different stories.

One difference was they were not brothers, they were cousins. More research, yes, they were brothers. Wesley had moved to Virginia before the war. William never forgave his brother for fighting with the Confederates.

X

They met in battle some time before Gettysburg, the battle at Winchester. The Union force was severely beaten. When Wesley found who the force was that they defeated, he went to where captured soldiers were being held. There, he found his brother, Captain Culp and so it was that the Captain asked his brother, Wesley to deliver the letter to his sweetheart thinking he most likely would not survive prison camp. (Few did). However, it was not long later, Captain Culp was released in a prisoner exchange and was walking home as the battle of Gettysburg was underway.

July 2, 1863 the Confederates are attacking Culps' Hill on the Culp farm. The Confederate forces were beaten back twice and they finally retreated. One of the fallen on Culps' hill was Wesley Culp with the undelivered letter. There is no proof, but it is widely believed that his sisters recovered his body and buried it. Quite possibly in the farm house basement. The stock of his rifle was later found with his name carved in it.

So it came to be that at Culps' hill the Civil War changed direction and headed South.

Search the internet, there is a whole lot of information about The Culp family that came to the United States in 1744.

Paul and Jim

Just for background, let me introduce my two BFFs, Jesus Christ and God Damn It. Their real names were Paul and Jim. I said their first names were Jesus Christ and God Damn It because that's what I heard them called by their Dad.

We were boys of action. So many a day, their dad would come home from work, take one look at what we were doing, look at Paul and say 'Jesus Christ', take another look at our work then turn to Jim and say, 'God Damn it'. At this point I would usually say 'I have got to go home now'.

Chapter 1

The Farm

Our farm was my father's dream. I am happy to this day that he had a dream. Growing up there, I thought I was such a hick. I was so jealous of my cousin that lived in the city. He could walk to the movies and do things I could only imagine. I couldn't wait to get off the farm. I finally did and so I have spent the majority of my life wishing I could go back.

Today, I realize I would not trade my youth for anything. Thanks Mom & Dad.

Our farm was not large by any means. It was however big enough to have pheasants, rabbits and the elusive muskrat for a farm boy and his friends to pursue. At the far end of our farm was a pond that held a fair number of Bullhead catfish. Many memories from that pond. Much more fun than any 'Play Station' game.

The farm was the closest farm to town. In fact, the whole farm was within the town limits. The rear of the farm was bordered by the New York Central Railroad. The farm and that pond was OUR internet. Every summer day, it was baseball, the pond or the farm. Lots of friends. Many are still friends. That does not happen with city people.

The farm had the classic red barn with a double pitched roof on each side. This made for much more hay storage in the upper floor aka "Hay Loft". Later, it was cleaned out to become a basketball court. Many nights were spent playing there in the winter.

The 'hay loft' had a sliding white door on the front with the name "Poplar Farm" in bold block letters. This because we had three of the biggest poplar trees I have ever seen.

I should also add that the 'Barn' was where I had my first close encounter with a girl. Relax, not much happened because neither of us had any idea of what to do about the biological changes that were happening to us. True to my promise to her, her name remains sealed forever. The memory of her is still vivid. **Coming of Age** for sure.

I learned to drive on the farm starting with a tractor. My Dad was really happy when I started driving the tractor because many jobs were much easier with two people.

Farmall Super A

I was really young. My dad adjusted the seat all the way forward and even sitting on the very edge of the seat, I could not reach the peddles. Dad, being a carpenter, fashioned big blocks of wood to attach to the clutch and two brake peddles. It worked. I pretty much had to stand on my right foot so I could depress the clutch with my left foot.

I became quite proficient. Soon I was plowing, cultivating and all the jobs done by tractor. I hated picking fruit etc. and would go to great lengths to duck those jobs.

When it came to driving a tractor with real power under you, I was there sun up to sun down. Never an argument. My dad would never pay me to help him and I never asked. If I worked exceptionally well and my dad was pleased, the next morning I would find his pocket change in my shoe. Made me happy, that's for sure.

I am not sure what caused the change in my dad, but later in life, he would see my boys and the first thing he would do was to pull out his wallet and say, "Let's see what Grandpa has in here for these boys." He would give out five dollar bills! The same man that slipped me pocket change. Go figure.

On our farm, we grew most everything and being in the North, everything grew fast including weeds.

Grapes was our biggest crop. Concord Grapes. Tons of them. In the early years, we contracted with Welch's Grape Juice. Later years we sold to Chateau Gay winery.

The farm also had a racetrack of sorts. Quite small because the only race car was a tractor. There was a section of the farm that had very soft sandy loam soil. This is where we grew our personal produce. Potatoes, sweet corn, tomatoes, peppers , onions, melons, you name it. Around this area was the race track.

Much fun there. Tied with a rope behind the tractor would be a surf board (just a piece of wood actually) or perhaps an old car hood to perform like a boat when inverted. Kids would pile on and away we would go as fast as the tractor would go. Round and round. Fall off and you had to run really fast to get back on. I am pretty sure no one was killed.

Cutting diagonally across the farm was a small creek that was dry most of the year but was a torrent during spring runoff. On occasion, it was home to the elusive muskrat.

Flame Out

One summer day My Dad was working the area enclosed by my race track. He heard a jet passing overhead. Nothing unusual about that. It was a regular feature living only 15 miles from Niagara Falls Air Force base.

This one was different. About the time it got directly overhead, it went silent. What? My Dad looked up and he saw a T-33 jet trainer headed north toward Lake Ontario. Odd that it was so quiet.

Dad starts back to work and he hears a POP. Now what? He looks up again and here is a pilot in a parachute coming down. He's still way up there, but it's looking bad for our tomato plants.

This was not one of the modern square parachutes that you could steer, it was big. Like you might see in a World War II movie. He began drifting to the south. Now it looks like he's going residential. He missed Main street by a small amount and landed behind Ed's Garage. A couple of bruises but he was okay. The T-33 made a really big hole in Milton's pasture. No animals were harmed or injured making this movie...

This is where I had my **"Coming of Age"**..

That is a brief look at where I grew up. A Google map 'Earth View' of 2660 New Road, Ransomville NY will give you a view of the farm. It is rather hard to determine the boundaries now because many houses have been constructed.

Chapter 2

Paul

I am sitting here at this keyboard struggling to write about my friend because I miss him. He was the first of our threesome to go. He did not deserve to be the first to go. He didn't smoke or drink.

You just don't know when it is time. I guess it's best that way.

Paul and I were really close friends for a lot of years. I was a mere four days older than Paul. How long were we friends? I used to ride my tricycle to his house. His house was not next door, it was a substantial ride.

Bud & Paul

We did almost everything together, hide and seek, red light green light, baseball, hunting & fishing and later on we even dated girls that were cousins. He married one of them.

Many crazy times with cars that we should not have survived. I remember the old guys at the gas station saying neither one of us would see 25. He was the first of our gang to own a '55 Chevy. Dark blue and fast. I remember one time he was going the usual speed, wide open, and there was a tremendous Bang! Out of reflex, he ducked. When he straightened up, he couldn't because the roof was on his head. What? UH OH, where did the hood go. Looking back, there it was floating back down above the power lines.

One time, he came to the farm, and backed his mother's car all the way into our barn. The floor in the barn was just gravel. When he made his exit, it was at full throttle. Nothing but dust and rocks flying everywhere. A true sight to see.

Late in our High School years, Paul would drive his mother's '54 Chevy. It would do 94 mph on the flat. More about that later.

Paul used to swipe KOOL cigarettes from Johnston's, his uncle's restaurant. Then we would smoke them in the woods at the chicken farm. That meant we were KOOL.

I actually did not start smoking until I was a senior in High School. It was at rehearsal for the Senior play. During breaks, the girls would go outside to smoke. I got invited to join and that did it. A lot easier starting than quitting.

So Paul & I did a lot together including flirting with a couple of girls from Ransomville. that went on for a long time. I have heard that they still ask about me.

After I started high school, my Mom went back to work. That left a lot of free time for me. One day, a car pulled in the driveway. A woman got out and said she was looking for her daughter, one of the girls previously mentioned. Have I seen her? No. A few more questions and she leaves. Both of the girls were hiding in my bedroom closet ! Most certainly **'Coming of Age'**.

There were times Paul and I didn't get along so well. As with most friendships, there were things that happened to test that friendship. One of those times came when Paul nearly chopped my fingers off with a meat cleaver. I never really blamed him for that one. More about that when you read about Doctor Piazza.

The time he really tested our friendship was on opening day of pheasant season. I had been doing preseason scouting as usual and I had located a place where the pheasants roosted every night. One evening I had seen a pheasant gliding into this area to spend the night. I spent a few nights watching the area and after a short number of days, it was easy to tell, this was THE HOTSPOT. Every evening, birds would come cruising in from all directions. What a Jackpot. The whole area was declared off-limits by me.

When Pheasant season came, I told Paul and Jim that I had the spot. Opening day we are at the farm house a good hour before sun-up. Pumped up with excitement.

The trouble begins. Paul says, "Let's go." What? No-way, it's still dark. Minutes pass. Let's go. NO. More minutes pass. Come on, let's go. **NO NO NO.**

More minutes pass, faint light. **LET'S GO.** Big mistake, I give in. Heinous Error and I knew it. But, there we go, ready to launch the attack.

The plan was that we would sort of surround the birds so they would have to flush and not run. We got in position and closed in. Big Big mistake, we could barely see each other.

The birds start flushing . Is that a rooster or a hen? Can't tell. No shot. More flushes really close Hen? Rooster? Nobody knows and so it went, lots of birds, no shots fired so naturally, there was **ZERO** kills. I was so pissed at Paul, I wanted to stuff him in my game pouch.

I never forgave him for that until, well, right now. I guess it was a **Coming of Age** moment.

Bad News

Autumn of 2013, I was packing my gear to do the Camino de Santiago in Spain. It is a pilgrimage that starts in France and you trek all the way across Northern Spain to Santiago where St. James is buried. That is when Jim called to tell me that Paul had the Big C diagnosis. I wanted to cancel my trip, but Jim said he was doing good. I said I would fly up as soon as I got home.

I was in Spain for a month. Walking the Camino, you carry a stone with you that you put your Life burdens on and you leave that stone and your burdens at The Cruz de Ferro (The Cross of Iron) I carried three stones, one for me, one for my son and another for Paul. Being older now, I try to be 'Manly', but I totally fell apart there.

Upon my return from Spain, I repacked and two days later, I was in Ransomville to visit my friend. One of the hardest things I have ever done. Try to remain upbeat when you know the Grim Reaper is at hand. We had a good time talking about 'Old Times'.

Getting ready to leave to return to Texas, Paul asked if I would come back in the spring to go Salmon fishing. You bet I said. He smiled at that. We said our Good byes. It was easy for me to see that this was **THE** Goodbye.

The next morning Jim took me to the airport and it was a long thoughtful ride to Corpus Christi.

That evening, they took my friend to the hospital and he passed away only a few hours later.

I am thinking he hung on until I got there, just for me.

I miss you Hound Dog.

Three Friends
November 11, 2013

Chapter 3

Jim

Jim, aka Fenimore, in later years was trouble more often than not when we did things together. Today, we still see each other from time to time because both of his children have become Naturalized Texans. His daughter Beth lives in Houston and his son Jim, lives in Austin.

When we can coordinate timing, we get together and go up to our farm in Rockdale to shoot guns and fish. We have a nice sheltered lake and we both love to fly fish.

Before we married our wives, the girls were roommates in the city. Our firstborn children were born on the same day, in the same hospital. Rather amazing.

Jim is the youngest of our threesome and he reminds me of that. The bottom line is, he is losing his hair, I am not. Ha

Where to start? I have promised not to 'Tell All'. So, I will tell only good things we have done **if I could just think of one.**

I remember a time when we stopped at the Porter Hotel for a beer. It turned out the owner had gone somewhere and left this kid to run the Bar. It got pretty rowdy as the night progressed and the kid was losing control. There was a back room that had tables where a family could sit. I never saw a family in there but sometimes overflow drinkers would be there.

A scheme developed where someone would ring the buzzer in the back room that would sound in the bar area signaling the bar keep that someone needed service. When the buzzer sounded, the kid would head that way. Whoever was standing at the far end of the bar would simply open the cooler there and hand out beer. When the kid came back, someone would carry some of the free beer to the back room. Sweet.

At closing time, 2am, the kid says he's closing. He was informed that was not to be. Way too much fun. The party continues for quite some time until Jim says "UH OH", two of his favorite words.

There standing outside (the door did get locked) looking in the door window was a guy wearing a smokey bear hat and he didn't look like he was about to party. Jim, at the far end of the bar, bolts for the back door in the store room. I am in hot pursuit. The back stairs were Jim's demise.

He takes a header which was good for me because bear #2 has just arrived and quickly bends and grabs Jim. I am AIRBORNE and clear both of them. I was the only one to escape. I think they felt sorry for the kid because the highway patrol guys let everyone go anyhow. Never saw that kid work there again.

The Bankers Turn

In the same time frame as above, arguments started about the main intersection in town that was controlled by our sole blinking traffic light. This intersection was also known as 'The Four Corners'. Clever. The corners were as follows. Northeast was Coddy's corner store. Southeast corner was Shorty's gas station. Southwest was Burly's store. Northwest was the old bank bldg, then a store of sorts operated by Beete McCormack. Today, it is once again a Bank.

What was special was the tightness of the corner. The only thing between the street and the old bank was a narrow sidewalk. Coddy's store sat back a few feet, but there was a telephone pole at the very apex of the corner, not three feet from Ransomville road or Main street.

Now with that visual, the arguments start about how fast could you come from East on Main Street, and turn North onto Ransomville road without hitting the pole or the bank.

At this point, I assume there is a Statute of Limitations on things of this nature.

For some reason, Jim (a) trusted my driving ability (b) had too many beers or (c) was just crazy. He decided he would ride with me if I was going to attempt it. He would be a speed observer to settle any doubts or arguments about how fast the speed was.

So here we go. Spotters are out to insure there is no traffic coming. My hot rod Chevy is pulsing and throbbing with it's race cam in front of the American Legion Building about a quarter mile away. There's the signal. We're off, fifty MPH. Steady, steady, hard right to get the car into a slide. The rear bumper misses the gas pumps at Connor's Gas station easily. The slide is perfect. Hard on the gas again, the front bumper misses the telephone pole. Tires are cooking now. The rear bumper misses the Bank. Recover from the slide and away we go. Just way too easy.

After a consultation, it was decided I could do better. Better we did. The final analysis was, the "Bankers Turn" could be done at 70 miles per hour. At that speed, the margin of error on the three key areas, the entry, mid curve and exit was very small. I did it on numerous occasions usually to the cheers of friends. Jim almost always was my copilot. I often wonder if that trick is still being attempted and did anyone ever top it?

The 'Four Corners' had a **Coming of Age** and was renamed 'The Bankers Turn'.

Some years later, I sold my beloved '55 Chevy. Still with no dents. What was I thinking? If only we could make those choices again.

THE COLD WAR

About to be drafted, it was decision time. I was invited to take my induction physical, which I was told was perfect. So the clock is ticking. The thoughts of infantry in the Army was not too appealing.

All of my side of the family had been in the Air Force so I went to talk to them. They said I did great on my testing so I could go into any field they had openings in. Off We go into the Wild Blue Yonder, Flying High yada, yada. I received my Draft notice for the Army while I was at Basic training in the Air Force. That was close.

Jim elected the Marine Corps. A family tradition for him.

Fast forward to October 1962. Does it mean anything to you? It meant a lot to Paul, Jim and myself. Not wanting to miss the pheasant season, Jim and I took leave to be home for the event. We made our connection in Ransomville and hit the fields for opening day. That evening, I turn on the TV and there is JFK saying that Russian missiles en route to Cuba is an act of war and that they will not reach Cuba.

There they are on a Russian ship with a U.S. Navy destroyer along side.. Holy Crap.

The next morning, Jim said, "Did you see TV last night?" I said, "I hope we have a good hunt today", thinking it could be the last one.

At lunch time that day, we stopped at Johnston's Restaurant for lunch. Edna, the owner saw us and came hustling over saying I was to call home immediately.

Jim and I both looked at each other knowing what this meant. Mom knew our routine and she knew where we would be at lunch time. I called home and Mom was really upset. She said there was a telegram for me. What does it say? She said she didn't know because it (the telegram) was for me. For Pete's sake Mom, open it!

The wording was different than I had expected but it was the same thing. Report back ASAP, respond ASAP with flight plan, arrival time etc, etc. Jim and I looked at each other and I said I hoped we would get to see each other again. The Russians had been stewing for a fight for a long time. JFK said here we go.

We knew this was it. Jim got his telegram that evening. We said goodbye that night and we truly thought it was **THE GOODBYE**. Later, those ships turned around, I couldn't believe it.

This was a huge **'Coming of Age'** moment for both of us.

TEXAS

Years later, I got Jim up to the farm in Texas to hunt and fish. It was quite a surprise to him. He was thinking West Texas desert-like terrain, not rolling wooded hills that were green. He loved our lake that had a lot of good sized Bluegills. Great sport for a fly fisherman.

On his first trip, I introduced him to BBQ. Not just BBQ, but **BBQ** From Texas. I took him to Mueller's BBQ in Taylor, Texas. Always listed by the experts as being in the top Five in Texas. Naturally, that puts them in the top five in the world. Need I say more?

We get to Mueller's and it is HOT. Hot enough to do some crotch pot cooking. Big line, it is Saturday. Weekdays are advised. It took 45 minutes in line to place our order. This place is OLD. No a/c, no nothing. Everything looks the same, smoke colored from the cooking operation. The menu is written on a piece of meat wrapping paper, also in earth tones.

Half way through the order line, Jim is staring at a big picture on the wall of Guy Fieri. He does a 360 and says, "I saw this place on the Food Channel!" Yep. Jim asks what to order? I told him to order a Brisket sandwich. For a novice, you can't go wrong The aroma in there is a killer, by the time we got our order, we were hungry.

We found a small table in the overflow area, eating begins and I look up to see Jim staring at me. What? He says quite loudly, **"THIS IS THE BEST ROAST BEEF I HAVE EVER TASTED!"** A hush falls over the eating area. Heads turn and people stare. Where did you find this guy? It's Brisket Baby!

Since that day, I have also taken him to Snow's BBQ, another in the top 5. Now the priorities have changed when we are together. It is now BBQ, fishing then shooting.

All through our teen years, I thought I was the best shooter with any firearm. After his Marine Corps training, I have to admit he is better than me at least with a rifle. On one of our last outings, he was shooting my 45-70 rifle in a severe crosswind. At one point, from 100 yards, he put three consecutive bullets through the same hole. Doubt it? Check the video that can be seen on YouTube. Search for theflycaster (all one word) on YouTube and you can see many videos of our shooting and fishing. Click on my channel and see a lot of my travel, plus our farm.

You will find more stories in this book featuring adventures with Jim. Many are funny except for the one where he **shot me.**

Chapter 4

Grade School

Ransomville Union School. I never did understand the 'Union' part, but I guess it meant a lot to someone. Grades 1-8. No Kindergarten in those days. All classes in 4 classrooms. first & second in one room, third & fourth in another etc. How can this be?

To give you a better picture, there were only nine kids in my graduating class, seven boys and two girls.

Early on, I noticed that I was the youngest in my class. This would be significant in the coming high school years when the girls in my class were two years older than me. What's two years? It's like 20 years when you are older. A huge disadvantage in sports also. A sixteen year old competing with eighteen year old boys for a spot on a team is tough.

Girls driving cars and me riding a bicycle............. not pretty. So there I am flirting with sophomore girls that were my own age and I was a senior. Not fair.

The meanest bully in our class was Bummer. He like the rest, was two years older than me and twice my size. I was quite sure I would never make it to high school. My savior was Kenny. Not that he protected me, it was just that Bummer liked to pick on him more than me. Kenny survived also. In fairness, it wasn't just Kenny and I that got abused by Bummer the Bully. My friend Dave and his wife Sandy and several others that have been sources for this book, have been relating stories of the times they were also bullied. More about that later. Fear, that will give you a **'Coming of Age'** awakening.

Tough Teachers

Our 3rd and 4th grade teacher was tough. If there was any mischief, she would catch the culprit every time and do it quickly. We were certain, she had, 'Eyes in the back of her head'. She could be writing on the chalk board when a disturbance occurred and she would turn and go right to the perpetrator and serve the punishment she deemed appropriate.

I considered this phenomena for some time until I was certain I knew how she did it. I decided it was worth a test. Gary, the smartest in our class, sat directly behind me. He was to be the test animal. Our teacher turned her back and I summoned all my courage and chunked a paper wad at a kid on the other side of the room.

Much laughter. I knew what was coming so I quickly spun around and stared at Gary. I was really tense when I heard her coming, thinking I may have miscalculated, but she cruised right by me and gave Gary a whack with a ruler.

Gary, being true to the code of honor didn't point and say, 'It wasn't me, he did it'. So much for "Eyes in the back of her head". Mission accomplished.

Gary, I am sorry I got you a ruler lick.

Memories

One of my favorite memories was when I got every kid in the school a day off and I didn't get punished.

Seventh grade science 'show and tell' with Nature as the theme. I had a brilliant idea. On the other side of the road from the farm was a wood lot about a quarter of a mile away. I trekked back to the woods to begin my search, I knew just about where it was.

I spotted it, a huge Paper Wasp nest that was reachable from the ground. It was mid winter so there was no danger. In the summer time, we used to chunk rocks at them until one of us would get stung. It's kind of like they were unhappy about having their home destroyed. Go figure. We called them 'Black Jacks' because they were black and BIG.

I got the nest, including the branch it hung on. First prize for certain. On Friday, my dad actually drove me to school to deliver my 'Show & Tell' project. The norm was to walk to school in the winter and ride a bike during warmer times. Walking a mile in mid winter could be brutal.

As predicted, my Paper Wasp nest won the prize. It was a beautiful specimen about the size of a basketball only more of an oval shape. No breaks or tears in the nest. It was perfect. I was a proud kid.

The following Monday was a different story.

We got to school and were greeted outside by the teachers. The school was closed for the day. Come back tomorrow they said. It developed that my entry into the contest had a second lesson. This lesson was about hibernation of various species. In this case, paper wasps, about a thousand of them.

When they were captured, it was mid winter and they were sound asleep. Due to a surprise warm spell (the classroom), the wasps woke up and decided that summer had arrived very early this year. Out they came ! The search for food was on. Being trapped in a school building did not provide much food for them. By Monday morning, the wasps were rather irritated. And so, it was a day off for all the kids.

I don't think any of the students congratulated me for such a grand feat....... not a single one of them !

The Pumpkin Caper

Some teachers just never learn. This time we were approaching Halloween and so there was a Pumpkin show organized. Most original etc. etc. My artistic talents were average at best so I knew the prettiest etc. was not within reach.

I did however have one big advantage, We **GREW** pumpkins. Hundreds of them. My target was the Biggest ! I found one that was so big, there was no way for me to get it to school much less, out of the field. Dad rescued me and the Great Pumpkin with the tractor and a trailer.

The carving was just so so. But the sheer size made it a certified winner. Once again, Dad to the rescue. I was a bit nervous about my dad bringing the pumpkin into the classroom because I was afraid the teacher who was also the Principal would say something like, "While you are here, I would like to talk to you about a couple of matters involving your son".

That didn't happen. I'm thinking she was overwhelmed by the great pumpkin. It was grand indeed. She wanted to place it on a bookcase and to do so, the bookcase had to be pulled about a foot further away from the wall. I think by today's standards, there would be some kind of OSHA law suit over that. There sat the Grand Pumpkin casually leaning on the wall, Grinning at all the kids and their feeble entries into the contest.

Skip forward a period of time. We show up for class on a Monday to hear of a death in the family. The Great Pumpkin had died or at least his back half had died and fallen behind the bookcase. The first time I had seen a corpse and it wasn't pretty. I think the janitor, Herman, said it's not his problem, so some of the boys were ordered to help me get the Cadaver to the Morgue. Gag me.

A congressional order was issued the following year, there would be no prize for the largest pumpkin. How sad !

Sports

Sports in our grade school consisted of recess and some choose up sides baseball. No coach, no nothing. Just have fun kids.

We were okay with that until one day we found out that we (not sure who 'We' meant) were going to put together a team to play basketball against the kids from Wilson. You have to be joking. That's like putting PEE WEE football kids up against The Green Bay Packers ! And so it happened. The child abusers came to town and abused the kids from Ransomville. This was the first time I got to see Arnie in action. He was better than all the other kids from Wilson by a wide margin. When we got to high school, he was like all World everything, at least that's the way the girls saw him.

Who would do a thing like that? I'm thinking the Principal, Lydia, who lived in Wilson did this to get even for the grey hair we gave her. Like the time three of us stretched a piece of clothesline across the road by the farm. It was only a foot off the ground. No big deal Trouble started that night when the first car that came by was Lydia ! She MADE it a BIG DEAL. Tires squalling and she spotted us. There was a Royal Ass chewing the next school day. Grey Hair for her!

Lydia was tough. I remember her dragging a boy to her office for disciplinary work and I saw him wet himself. I will not mention his name. No, it was not me.

I remember how embarrassing it was when she would walk into the shower room when we were in the showers. I am thinking she would be on the local news channel if she did that today.

So ends the Grade School sports stories.

Today, I understand that it truly was COOL that there were only nine kids in my class.

20

Chapter 5

Trapping

In the days before the advent of the Internet, X-box and Video in general, We were OUTDOOR kids. Trapping animals was a huge part of our activities. I have to admit that we pretty much sucked at it. The prime fur was muskrat.

The fur of a muskrat is very comparable to that of a mink. It is extremely soft and is an awesome insulator for wintertime. In the era of the 40's & 50's, almost all ladies coats would have muskrat fur collars and/or cuffs. Many gloves that were 'High End' would be muskrat lined. This afforded a big market for us to sell furs to a commercial buyer.

Like I admitted, we pretty much sucked at the trapping for a living idea. A half dozen furs was a good season.

There was however one of the guys that we 'hung' with that was good at it. Like a poker player, He was 'All In' when it came to the outdoors. His name was Eddie and he was number one when it came to hunting and fishing.

Eddie

So with humble respect, I will share a couple of funny stories about my now departed friend Eddie who was so intense about the outdoors, he became known as, "Field and Stream". How's that for a nickname? R.I.P. Eddie.

The first story was fishing at our favorite fishing hole, the Cold Storage pond. A pond that had been used in the pre- refrigeration days as an ice supply for the storage of apples etc. That was before our time, so the pond no longer had commercial use. It then became a fishing hole for us boys. It was OUR internet. It contained enough Bullhead Catfish to keep us entertained. Most were between 6 and 8 inches in length.

The funny part was watching Field and Stream in action. Our fishing rigs were quite a bit less expensive than today's gear. A simple fishing rod and reel with no elaborate drag system, a hook and a sinker. Add a juicy night crawler that we caught ourselves and you were set.

Often, it was a long time between bites so we would cast the bait out, prop the rod up on a stick and tell stories etc. while watching the rod tip. When the rod tip of Field and Stream's rod wiggled, it was time to get out of the way. He would rush to it but not touch it. He would position his feet, just so, then place his hands around the pole without touching it. The next 'twitch' of the pole would trigger an explosion few fishermen have ever experienced. A truly violent RIP of the rod and Eddie would be running in high speed reverse reeling at a speed never seen before. Not very much 'Playing' the fish, closer to water skiing for the fish I would say. I always thought one day he would reel in only the jaw bone of a 6" fish. You had to be there to understand.

Eau de Perfume

The next 'Field & Stream' story is trapping. No, not Muskrats, SKUNKS. Eddie was good at it, but with trapping a skunk, there is one Big Problem. They can be very unkind to you if you corner them and a trapped skunk is most definitely cornered.

Eddie lived in a house that was right next to the Grade School. Grades 1 thru 8. No Kindergarten in those days. On this particular day, everyone could tell from a great distance that Eddie had indeed 'cornered' a skunk. Our Principal promptly sent him home with directions to Clean up. When he returned, it was worse ! A "Gag-Me" concoction of Eau de Polecat & Eau de cheap aftershave. Sent home with orders to try again the next day.

Even after that, Eddie always had hopes of taming a skunk for a pet. He should have never mentioned that to me. I even dabbled in skunk trapping without success UNTIL..... It was the last day of trapping season, the 28th of February and it was a Saturday so I set off to pull up my trap line. Near the end, I got to the Chicken Farm. There was a long building that turkeys were raised in. The ground floor was an open basement of sorts. Doors and windows missing and pretty much full of junk.

If you look in one of the windows, there was an area just wide enough for a skunk to pass through along one wall. A perfect spot for a trap. I looked through the "non existent" window and BINGO, I had caught a Beauty. Angry, but odor free. Now what? Get Eddie of course. I ran into town (a short run) and found Eddie and the guys doing nothing in particular. I told the story and he wanted to know if you could get to it for a 'Live' capture, obviously hoping that maybe if I was a true friend, I might let him capture it for himself.

The reason he didn't already have one for a pet was because they were normally caught in a hole and would have to be killed to get them out.

So here comes a posse of about 10 boys, hell bent on the live capture of a skunk. Yes, we found out what Hell was that day. Eddie sees it and decided it would be an awesome pet. I said, "If you can do it, it's yours". The planning starts but there is no good plan. About that time , a man that worked at the chicken farm walked up and asked what we were up to. We showed him the skunk and he agreed it was a fine looking skunk.

He told Eddie that it was not difficult to capture a skunk without the atomizer going off. Really? He said sure, if you can get close enough and you pick up the critter by the tail, he can't spray.

Seriously? Yep, some of you kids distract the Skunk, and one of you sneak up behind him. Okay, let's do it. So we, the distraction team, run a long board through the window and begin bouncing it. No doubt, we had the attention of that skunk.

Now here comes Eddie behind a big piece of cardboard. It is very obvious that the skunk is fully aware there is a something coming closer from the other direction also. Closer and closer. Bounce the board more. He's right there. WOW, I can't believe this. Eddie starts peeking over the top sizing up his opponent. Bounce goes the board. The skunk checks it.

Eddie drops the cardboard and makes a grab as sure as the best shortstop in all of the Major Leagues. Eddie jumps up holding the skunk by the tail and SQUEALS , "I got him!"

Umm, not so fast Eddie, The skunk has you. With equally fast action, Eddie chunks the skunk some where and comes tearing out of that building discarding clothing way faster than any stripper I have ever seen.

Remember, it was the last day of February and that was before Global Warming. You know, it was the kind of day when it was so cold, the snow would squeak when you walked on it. Some of you will not understand that. You will just have to trust me, if it is cold enough, snow squeaks when you walk on it.

The last I remember was the worker walking away shaking his head mumbling something about Damn fool kids.

I was quite some distance from where the aroma was generated, but when I got home my mother sent me straight to our basement to 'Get Naked', then straight to the bath. I couldn't smell it. I guess I was sweet compared to Eddie.

My Boys Learn to Trap

Skipping forward a few years (like 40) my two sons and I were pretty heavy into fishing and hunting. The oldest, just becoming a teenager. The younger about to become one. A proud father watching the boys developing skills with a fishing lure and firearms.

They were always asking questions about my youth in the outdoors. They always enjoyed my stories and I told the truth, **mostly**. Admittedly, I eliminated some of the dumber things I did as a stalker of game.

Because of tales told of trapping, my youngest was very interested in this activity. Thus I made a serious error. That Christmas I bought him a trap. A Victor 1-1/2 single spring. New and shiny from the hardware store. On Christmas Day, there was no greater gift that I could have given. He treasured it

Now the questions came like a flood. How, what, where, when ? More and more questions. Now, keep in mind, we lived in a small city. He pointed out to me there was a public swimming pool nearby that had a small woodlot behind it. Would there be anything there Dad?

Sure I said , it's probably loaded with marten, mink, badger, possibly a mountain lion or two and most certainly raccoon. The oldest son rolled his eyes but the younger was Gung-Ho to catch a Raccoon.

After some basic instructions, I was confident he would not trap his own fingers. Off he went with all his gear, a hatchet, his one trap and a can of stinky sardines.

24 hours later, home from school, the door flies open and a young Boy is yelling, "I GOT ONE". Back out the door in a flash. Thirty minutes later, he's back with a raccoon. What a boy, what a great teacher! Ha. Oh boy, what have I done? Now it's time to teach him how to skin the critter and prep the hide. Where are you going? I asked as he headed out the driveway. "Gonna catch another one Pop".

24 hours later, raccoon # 2 is in the garage. Can you show me again how to skin one? You might by this time see where this is going.

Another 24 hours passes. The boys burst in excitedly saying "We got a BIG one". It indeed was. It was a large black tip (meaning the fur ends were very black) Male. One of the best I had ever seen.

A Black Tip !

Another 24 hours passes. The young one bursts in saying (I'll never Forget it) "You're not going to believe this Dad, but I got a FOX !". Oh my, what have I done? A FOX ? We live in a city ! A FOX? You gotta be kidding............ Nope, it was a beauty.

The Hunters

And so it went. Not long later, I got the boys up early on a Saturday because I had located a buyer that would be at a feed store in a town 20 miles away. They had spent a lot of time grooming those Furs. They were rolled up and frozen until sale day.

There were a lot of so called trappers there and looking around, I could see a lot of BAD quality furs there. I saw one Raccoon that I swear had 500 shotgun pellet holes in it. I am certain a number were "Road Kill". Never the less, a line formed and one by one the 'Trappers' climbed the stage to collect their bounty. The boys were about 5th in line. Just before them a guy had what was supposed to be a fur. The buyer took a quick look and said, "get yourself and that stinking rag out of here!".

The buyer looked out at the sellers and said, "do not bring rotting flesh up here, **EVER!**" The line suddenly had fewer sellers. He looked back at the line and said, "come on up here boys, what have you got for me?" The boys flopped their hides on the table and the man said, OMG , He grabbed a couple of furs and holding them high in the air exclaimed, "see this boys? This is what I want to see!" These boys are going to make money today !"

They surely did, Remember that beauty that was caught on day #3? They sold it for $35.00. What ? I was thinking more like $5. A while later, there was a lull in the buying, so I asked why $35.00 ? He said that prime

raccoon fur was being exported to Japan. They could not get enough to meet their market demand. Never again would the pricing be like that. I often wondered, if the buyer paid $35, he probably sold it to a company that would then ship the furs to Japan. My thinking puts the Japanese value well in excess of $100.00.

So we get back in the truck to head home. I think both boys were 6 inches taller. Gotta admit , Dad was walking proud also.

Next was the bad news, well sort of......... Dad, can we stop by Jack's on the way home? Jack's is a truly amazing (sort of) hardware store. You name it, He's got it. (if he can find it). Why do you want to stop there? To buy more traps naturally. So it began...... getting up at 3am to run a trap line with the boys by boat on the Bayou then off to work by 7am. Even on weekends. No sleep-ins for trappers.

It was a fun time with those boys and it was financially sound. The money split was easy, 50/50/0 . It's okay we became not only Father and sons, but three friends..... Love you boys.

Trapping at Grandpa's

Good times with my boys.
Love You !

Chapter 6

Baseball

A lot to say about the National Passtime. For the kids of Ransomville growing up, it was way more than a passtime. There was a time when a good bunch of us skipped high school to have a game behind the Volunteer Fire Dept.

The only spectator we had turned out to be our Guidance Counselor. I am thinking it seemed strange at the High School when 80% of the boys from Ransomville were sick on the same day. It was a fun day though. But I have jumped ahead.

My earliest memories of baseball was playing at Johnston's Restaurant. A small yard was plenty of space. A very refined ball park it was. First base was a tree, Second base a fire hydrant and third was a telephone pole. Home plate and the pitchers mound were nothing more than a bare patch of dirt caused by much abuse from kids. A lot like Yankee Stadium in our minds.

Our town had no organized sports of any kind for kids. No pee wee football, no little league, no hockey rink. No nothing. The school had a gym but it was only used during school hours. Eventually the school got a baseball diamond, sort of! Mostly mowed weeds and bumpy. A well hit ground ball was hazardous for the best of the infielders. I know from playing a lot at third base. I stopped many with my chest and various other body parts.

I had the honor of playing on the first organized team that Ransomville ever fielded. I am not sure who the founding Fathers were. I do remember Gentle's Hardware and Gates Lumber Yard donating two brand new baseballs for every game. That WAS a big deal. Hoppy was our coach and I could probably name everyone on the team but I am afraid I would miss someone.

What an exciting time. We would practice for hours, then go to baseball **practice**. We knew we were going to be tough! Then it happened, our first game was to be a practice game in the city. Are we going to play a team from Niagara Falls? Yep.

Let me say right here, this was a time when if you were not good enough, tough luck kid, try again next year. No trophy that said 'Played' and everyone got one and no 5 run rule per inning. I remember two things from that game. First was Paul catching a line drive. I can still see it. That was the highlight reel. Simple, one line drive caught by my friend.

The most vivid memory however, was that the other team scored SEVENTEEN runs in the FIRST inning. Can you spell Child Abuse? We may have had something to do with the 5 run rule. Our pitcher didn't have his best 'Stuff' that day.

So from those beginnings, we started improving. Not surprising, we sure could not have gotten any worse. We even had a team Bus (of sorts) for a period of time.

A lot like our team Bus

Safarian's Sanitary Services let the team use an open Garbage truck to transport the team to away games. We started winning games. Maybe it was because we scared the hell out of other teams when they saw their opponents unload from a garbage truck. Sure wish I had film of that. Most of the trip, we had to keep your eyes shut because of the dirt and trash swirling around in that truck. We lost our team bus due to a Foul ball through the windshield. Safarian's said bye bye, find a different bus.

My Dad was a huge influence on my baseball playing. I would always tell him who we were playing and where it was at. Asking him if he was coming always got a no reply yet by the second or third inning, I would see him standing in the spectators. That was the Good news.

The Bad news was when I would make an error. I knew what was coming, rather I should say, I knew what was going. Just a glance and I would see my Dad walking toward the parking lot. **Man that hurt** ! It surely made me try harder.

An Intimidating Vision

One time, my whole family traveled to Cleveland by train to see a double header between the Yankees and the Indians. We rode the 'Nickle Plate railroad'. What a long day that was.

Wow, I remember well walking out the ramp to our seats. My first look at a major league stadium was intimidating. It must be a half mile from Home plate to the Center Field bleachers.

When the teams came out to warm up, I couldn't believe it. There stood a player or coach standing by the dugout hitting fly balls to the outfielders who were strolling around by the outfield fence talking to one another. These fly balls flew higher and farther than any baseball I had ever seen. It looked like the hitter was hardly swinging.

Dad explained it was because he was using a 'Fungo' bat. A trick bat. Wow, can I get one? Nope, they're illegal for play.

We had seats behind home plate in the upper deck looking straight down the base line toward first base. I can't remember hardly anything about the games or who won.   I do remember that in the second game, Mickey Mantle came to bat batting left handed. He got a pitch he liked and with a very loud crack, it was launched to right field and beyond. The hit was traveling straight away from me and I swear it was still climbing when it went into the upper deck. That vision is permanent.

Even though he was a Yankee playing against the Indians, He got a standing ovation for that one. What a shame that he drank himself to death later in his life.

After a few years, I started to pitch in some games. Not much of a curve ball, but I could bring the HEAT. (at least that's how I saw it)

When my dad learned that I was pitching some, he came home from work one day with a new catchers mitt. When he played semipro baseball in Florida, he was a catcher.

Nearly every evening before supper, my dad would catch me and on rare occasions give me a tip. But just like game time, if I threw just one wild pitch, he would get up from his position and head for the house, often without saying a word. The pitching ended because I was only good for six innings, anything more and it seemed like I was pitching watermelons. My pitches looked the same to the hitters also.

Our team stayed together through a couple of divisions until by age rule (15) we couldn't play anymore. Buy the end of it, we were a force to be dealt with, winning more game than we lost.

Then it was on to High School play, real uniforms! WOW, what a big deal that was. I got to be the starting center fielder and I wore #7 which was Mickey Mantle's number for the Yankees.

Coach Hutch was a great mentor to me. He must have thrown a thousand curve balls at me until I learned hit them. The Athletic fields at Wilson High School are now named after him. He was that kind of Coach.

R.I.P. Hutch

When I was in the military, I got an invite to come try-out for the base team. Yahoo, relief from basic training perhaps.

I was at tryouts for about an hour, Chasing down Fly-balls The others couldn't get to. I was running my ass off. I wanted to make this team.

Batting practice, my turn, I'm pounding the hits. This is looking good for me. Another guy steps in for his turn at bat. I'm behind the screen watching when I get to meet about 5 of the team regulars. Cool, not cool. They informed I would not make the team. You see, if I make the team, one of their friends goes Bye Bye. "We will break your arm if we have to. **Clear?"** Understood! I decided not to return for the second day even though I made the cut. No token white Dude for that team!

I wanted to be a Rocket Scientist anyhow.

Chapter 7

Dr. Piazza

Doctor Piazza came to town when I was quite young. He had a son John and a daughter Nancy. John was sweet on my sister for a while and one spring day he rode his horse to our house to impress my sister. The other thing he did was to ride his horse across our side yard, my ball field. The horse punched 6" deep holes all the way across. He was lucky he was not there when my dad came home. John became a business man of sorts, not very successful at anything I saw.

Nancy was kind of a Hottie, but she was always cold toward me so she missed out on a good thing.

I have one very vivid memory of the doctor. Paul, Jim and I were playing something, who knows what, part of the game was we were ransacking our club house. I grabbed this big wooden box to tip over at the wrong time because Paul had decided to hit the box with an old meat cleaver.

WHACK ! I looked down to see the index finger of my right hand hanging by the flesh on the underside of that finger. Had that cleaver been sharp, all the fingers would be gone.

This was also when I found out that your bones are not white like you find in a field perhaps. Instead, they are a very light pale green color. That really freaked me out.

My dad was called home from work and he took me straight to Doctor Piazza's office that was located in the front of his home. And there we sat. it was full of people.

Somewhere around 8pm people could see this kid was hurting so they gave their places in line to me. Now for the fun part, **NO anesthesia.** Dad held down my left side and the doctor sat on my right arm while he was putting my finger back together. There was a whole lot of screaming and I am sure some it was from me. I was sort of lucky if you will because the cleaver went through the solid bone just above the second knuckle. Had it been a bit further out, it would have gone through the knuckle and it would have been Bye Bye trigger finger.

When the Doc finished with me, Dad carried me out through the waiting room and I remember some people had faces as white as the paper I am typing on. There were no pain killers after my repairs either. I can still remember feeling every heart beat in my finger. That continued for a long time.

Today, my trigger finger points a bit to the right, but it still works. I was at the gun range with my grandson last Friday and I'll be going again this week. You bet I'm Pro Gun.

Black Cherries

On the West side of Dr. Piazza's house was a huge black cherry tree. In an orchard, the trees are trimmed every year to shape them so they grow wide and not tall. This is done to facilitate an easy harvest. Doctor Piazza's cherry tree had never been pruned so it was at least two times taller than the orchard variety. His tree had the sweetest cherries you could ever imagine. The amazing part was, he would let us kids at them. Wow, probably a dozen of us up there at a time. Some of us WAY up there. We knew where the sweetest fruit was. Can you imagine a Doctor allowing that today? None of the kids ever fell, no harm, no Foul.

Thanks Doc. It was indeed a Sweet time to grow up.

Chapter 8

Right from Wrong

My parents were an interesting couple. Mom was the Brains of the family and kept us financially secure. We were far from being rich, but equally far from being poor. Dad, was the A-typical German father, firm but never abusive. Rarely if ever voiced words of Love. He always had my respect. I never questioned his word. For example, at 8pm he would simply tell me, 'It's Bed Time' and I would never argue. Just off to bed. I often wondered how he did that, because there was always an argument from my boys...

I can only remember two times that I received physical punishment. Both well deserved. Here are those stories.

Fire in the Hole

Our big Red barn had a wing on one side that was used for Tractor and implement storage. The back half was used in the winter as a 'Brooder' room for newly hatched chickens. A 'Brooder' is a box affair that stands on legs about 4-6" off the floor. In the top of the brooder was a heater and a light. The opening around the bottom had little curtains to contain the heat inside and the chicks were free to come and go to feed and drink. This was the happiest time for a chicken.

When Spring arrived, the chicks would be feathered and moved to other locations to await their fate. The brooder was stored and the floor was cleaned of all the wood shavings and chicken residue. All that was left was a dirt floor and a hole in the roof with a tin chimney used for the heater.

The hole in the roof was my downfall. One nice summer day, a friend and I were playing in the barn. No video games then. I looked up and mentioned that I bet if you made a really smokey fire, the smoke would accumulate, then go straight out the chimney.

So on the dirt floor, a wooden box was placed and filled with a straw/hay mixture. I mentioned 'Dirt' floor to let you know I was not totally stupid. Strike a match and we had PLENTY of smoke. See, I told you. It's going out the chimney. Great celebration over a science project that was a success. **UNTIL...** I happened to look out the back window of the barn. A couple of hundred yards away was my dad. He was on the lane that ran the length of our farm. He was running, FAST. I had no idea my Dad could run that fast! Like a flash, we knew there was trouble with a capital **T**.

Out the barn we went and across the road. We dove into the high weeds just as Dad flew around the corner and into the barn. A long couple of minutes passed before my dad emerged. He was walking at a brisk pace and when he passed the door to the house and continued out the driveway, I thought this could be bad.

He reached down and picked up a stick. **UH OH**! He walked right to me and grabbed my collar. So much for my stealth. He proceeded to wail on my butt and let me tell you, it hurt. The only thing he said to me was 'Go in the house'. Not one word, then or ever about why I got the licking.

Not our barn, but it could have been.

'Put 'em Up!'

The other episode was in the same barn. A friend came over one day and he was all excited because he had some firecrackers that were freshly smuggled from Canada. You see, fireworks are strictly banned in New York. Because of this, a fire cracker was a treasure to us kids. They never last long, that's for sure.

Okay I know you are thinking these dumb kids are going to do something bad. You are correct. I saw my dad in the barn working on the tractor changing out an attached implement. Perfect! I had this cap gun and we could see that a fire cracker would fit perfectly in the barrel.

We used extreme caution sneaking up to the barn. Peeking around the door, there was dad, not 10 feet away. Perfect ! Light it, light it. The fuse roars to life. I step into the open, leveled the Pistol and said, "Hey Dad"? He looked up and said,'What?', just as an explosion **destroyed** my Cap Gun. Rib hurting laughter until the smoke cleared. My dad was **NOT** laughing.

It is right for me to mention here what a good man my father was to drop the big wrench he was holding.

Again, there was no explanation why my butt was so sore. The one with the fire I understood. A fun prank with a cap gun I did not.

Some 10-15 YEARS later, I had a dream about it and I sat right up in bed and I said to myself, "Holy Crap, my poor Dad thought I had SHOT him."

I'm sorry about that Dad. I'm thinking you should have killed ME.

Chapter 9

Winter in New York

In New York, there is not a whole lot you can do when the temperature drops to zero. It has been noted however that Child births are much greater in September October and November.

Being a kid was different. No TV to watch. Only one channel and it was only on part time. When it was on, a University of Buffalo 'Round Table' discussion of politics was somewhat less than exciting for kids, so it was back outside. We had our own games.

Lots of basketball in the barn. Bitter cold there, but the games played on. Our favorite fishing hole, the Storage Pond became our hockey arena. No boards around the rink, no nets, just us boys skating the best we could to get a puck or fake puck (crushed can perhaps) into the opponents goal, usually just an area marked with pieces of coal. Some of us had visions of playing for the Toronto Maple Leafs one day. Anything safety wise was non-existent. Many games ended when the first injury occurred.

Hooking Rides

The most fun any of us could have was "Hooking Rides" in the winter. The only gear required was a pair of hard soled shoes and a good pair of gloves plus a little nerve and some foot speed.

The first good snowfall that would "stick" on the roads would trigger this sport. Quite simple really, we would simply hang out at a street corner. When a car turned the corner, you would quickly run out behind the car or truck, squat down grabbing the bumper and off you went, skiing on your shoes. You were then "Hooking a Ride". At times, a car would go by with as many as four kids in tow. The worst position and the one most avoided was directly behind the exhaust pipe.

It was great fun. Old folks said it was dangerous because if the car hit the brakes you would go under and be killed. The truth was that if a 3000 pound car hit the brakes, any kid would stop long before the car. This was proven numerous times when people would stop as fast as possible to try to catch us. Every time, we would be long gone before they were out of the car. Simple physics, the laws of inertia, proven time and again by kids.

A real trip was when you would "Hook" one of the hot rod cars. If they saw you, they would gas it and take you on a real ride sideways etc.

The only real hazard would be if you hit a spot in the road that was 'Bare', causing your feet to stop at a bad time. Proper scouting would eliminate this problem. Railroad crossings could be a bit hazardous.

Years later, I was in the military stationed in Missouri. Not much snow there, but one night we were at the college campus (girls you see) when a rare snow storm hit. In a short period of time, several inches of snow had fallen.

A couple of cars doing donuts etc. and everyone was coming out for snowball fights etc. I mentioned the conditions were perfect for hooking rides. What ? No one ever heard of such a thing. For Pete's sake, let me out. They parked nearby to watch. Soon a car came around the corner. I shot out from behind some bushes and I was in heaven.

My first 'Hook' took me right by a Ladies dorm. Outside the girls were building snowmen etc. When I passed, some of them saw me and they yelled to their friends "Look at that guy"! Squeals of laughter and cheers for me, the guy on the back of a car waving at them to join me.

A few minutes later, my buddies were hooking all over the campus. Within a half hour, there was not a car anywhere without 2 or 3 students hooking or just plain being dragged everywhere. Sadly the snow pack was soon gone. I wonder if that tradition continues.

U.F.O.

In the late 1950's there had been a number of "UFO" sightings in our area. Everyone had an opinion. Most thought it was too much beer or bourbon. The people that said they saw them were generally thought of as weird people. Then it happened. I was on my way home after a date with my girlfriend. It was very late, maybe 1am on a very cold February night. I made the last corner before the farm and through the windshield, looking up about 45 degrees, there they were.

I am no artist, but this picture is very close to what I saw that night.

Four of them. At first, I thought they were fighter planes from the Air Force base with afterburners lit. But, they were not moving. I stopped the car and rolled the window down, thinking I would hear them. Nothing! Turn off the car, Silence! Whoa! A moment later, they moved and they moved FAST! They left in a Northeast direction and disappeared in only a second. Just four round circles that freaked me out. I did not sleep well that night and I never told anyone other than my friends what I had seen. Later I had heard others describing very similar sightings.

R.I.P. **Rod Serling**

Chapter 10

Bummer

Bummer, not as having a bad day or feeling sad, Bummer as a nickname for a kid from our town. Bummer was a big kid, bigger than any of us. Bummer was always angry for some reason. If you were smaller than him, you were in, "Harms Way". I was always certain he would kill me one day before I would reach maturity. I surely was threatened enough. A classic Bully.

I guess, I was lucky because Bummer had a favorite target, Kenny. Bummer would wail on him for the slightest reason. One day, much to our delight, he was beating on Kenny over nothing really when Alan, one age group above us saw what was happening. He asked Bummer, why he was beating on someone smaller than him, how about you and I get it on. Bummer says he has no fight with Alan. Alan says yes you do, I don't like to see big kids Bullying little kids and steps in. Bummer back peddles. Alan steps in more and there they go. Not in a fist fight, but a foot race. It was plain to see Bummer has his hand called and he wanted none of it. Just about the fastest I had ever seen Bummer run.

Gosh that was great. Bummer's threats didn't carry much weight after that day. It made me realize, I never once saw him pick a fight with anyone close to his size.

I did witness him abuse his sister once, right in front of a bunch of us boys. He thought it was funny. I knew if my dad ever saw me touch my sister like that, I would be dead. What's wrong with that kid?

There was a time we were at the ball fields behind the fire hall. Bummer had a hunting bow and there was a bunch of boys playing at the far side of the field diagonally from us. Beyond belief, he drew back the bow and launched an arrow at them. It was obvious the arc of the arrow was perfect. Much yelling by some of us, LOOK OUT, LOOK OUT! They all ducked and and the arrow struck right in the middle of all of those boys. Thank God, he missed them all. Holy crap. There was however, one big kid that thought it was funny. Those boys can all tell you it is impossible to see an arrow that is coming straight at you.

Bummer played on our baseball team and also in high school. He was our catcher and he could be mean. I remember a specific play once when we were still playing junior baseball. The team we were playing got this kid to third base. A rather smallish kid. Their next batter hits a sharp ground ball and the kid breaks for home. The play is at home, the kid is going to be out by a mile. Not waiting for the slide and an easy out, Bummer charges him and really flattens the poor kid. Easy to see, this kid is hurting. Then Bummer stands over the poor kid and celebrates. **I was ashamed of our team that day.**

On the lighter side, One spring day, we were playing by the creek bridge just down the road from the farm. Bummer had a new hunting shirt. One of those heavy duty wool shirts printed with big black and Red squares. Like the Arm & Hammer guy. Along comes Donnie, Clyde's older brother in his old Ford convertible. He stops to see what us kids were up to and Bummer jumps on the back bumper and starts bouncing. Donnie takes off but Bummer didn't jump off. A few seconds later, Bummer figures it out that he's going on a ride he does not want to go on. He steps off. Big mistake, the car is up to about 30 mph.

Bummer takes about three running strides in the neighborhood of 20 ft. per stride but his feet can't keep up. Lucky for him , he is angling toward a ditch as he crashes. He managed to climb out of the ditch, but his new shirt was destroyed.

Communicating with others from that time for this book, it has become quite clear that if you were younger and smaller than Bummer, sooner or later, you were going to be bullied, abused or humiliated by him. boy **or** girl. Thanks to those who came forward to tell of their belittlement at his hand. I thought he would surely kill someone one day.

Bummer is gone now. He was beaten by a **little guy**, a blood clot the size of a BB. I truly hope you have found peace Bummer.

Chapter 11

The Train

The New York Central railroad was the Southern border of our farm. The earliest memory I have of the railroad was seeing a 'Troop Train' that was passing through town. It stopped for a few moments and then moved on.

My Dad said the troops were headed somewhere to an Army post that I can't remember. I do remember all the soldiers leaning out of the car windows. They did not look happy. A couple waved to me. This was right at the end of WWII. I hope I wasn't the last person they waved to.

That may have been the only passenger train to pass through Ransomville. It surely was the only one I can remember.

The steam locomotives were so scary to us kids. The heat, noise and steam were to be feared. So the question was, how to get a ride. Quite simple really. The normal freight train would come through town twice a day. Eastbound around noon and Westbound around 10 pm.

One day the train pulled in to the station around noon. At that time of my life, you could still have mail and purchased items delivered by train. That was our UPS. On this particular day, the train pulled to a stop and the engineer looked down to see these three kids holding a substantial basket of fruit that was freshly picked at our farm. We held it up as an offering and the Engineer waved us up. It was HOT in that engine. We rode that engine on numerous occasions. He would let us ride around the town while he switched cars at a grain mill or lumber yard. All for the price of a basket of fruit. Sweet!

I have vivid memories of the heat that would hit us every time the fireman would step on a peddle to open the firebox to receive the coal that he shoveled. Really scary.

All too soon, the Steam locomotive was replaced by Diesel power and so the thrill was gone. It's just not the same.

Mixed Vegetables

The diesel train engine was one of those flat nosed switcher types made for a short haul.

It was nearly Halloween and the mischief was beginning. Wouldn't it be cool if that engine hit something like a pumpkin? There was a curve in the tracks near the farm that was selected because the engineer would not be able to stop once he spotted it.

The first attempt was less than exciting. It just barely hit the top of a pumpkin and it went under the engine. It was obliterated, but not very exciting. The solution? More Veggies! Yea! Just after dark we begin raiding a farm next to the tracks. This time, bigger is better. Pumpkins, all manor of melons, cabbages, corn, lettuce, you name it. A beautiful pyramid nearly four feet tall. Work was still in progress when we heard the train horn at a crossing in the distance. Run for cover!

Well hidden in a corn field, here she comes. She is moving fast. Had to be going at least **30 mph**. Yikes, can Veggies derail a train? Around the bend she comes. 50 feet from the pyramid, it is spotted. Full Horn blowing constantly. Boys needing an underwear change. **THUD!** No derailment. Thank you Lord. The train keeps going. I bet there was some serious talk, maybe laughter in that engine.

The next day, I snuck out to see the carnage. Yep, mixed veggies for a quarter mile. WOW. I had to hang around town that day for the train to come through. When it did, I was certain it was the same engine. It was well decorated with debris from the previous night.

In the event there is no Statute of Limitations on Heinous acts of crime on a railroad, I have not published the criminal's names in this story. Two of the Perps have passed on, but the remainder of us know who we are.

" ALL ABOARD "

Chapter 12

Halloween Mischief

Very early on in my life, Halloween was a much anticipated day to plan for every year. Not yet teenagers, the older generations knew we (meaning our Gang) would be a force to deal with. Mischief was way more fun than Trick or Treat.

A prime target was Out Houses. Yep, that's what I am talking about, one, two and the occasional three hole variety. I always wondered about the multi hole varieties. I hope it was because there were different sized holes. Who would want to be in there for business purposes with two other people. Yuk !

Mostly, the Mischief was tipping them over on Halloween night. I remember one such privy that we had dumped on a couple of occasions. That year during the Halloween scouting it was noticed that it sat quite close to a garage and the owner being tired of lifting the out house back into place, had anchored the facility to the garage with two lengths of threaded rod 3/8 inch in diameter.

Chuckles by all, it became target one. Come Halloween, the gang stalks in. No movement in the house.

First swipe with a hacksaw and the door flew open. Holy crapola, the guy was inside. A covey of quail/kids took flight. I bet he laughed for a long time.

Other privy capers took considerable planning because the plan was to burn them at an intersection of a street in our town. The Volunteer Fire Department thought this was great sport. There were only three or four intersections in our town, so it wasn't difficult to find the action scene.

The plan normally consisted of hijacking an old farm wagon. A lot were found in fields where they hadn't moved for years. Some times we would have to push it for a number of miles to the staging area. This was normally our farm due to the closeness to town. Then it was just a matter of backing the wagon up to the outhouse (very quietly) and tipping the facility onto the wagon and away we would go to the selected burn area.

BUSTED! Had to happen, I got caught attempting arson on a street corner. We had hijacked a privy using the method above. We planted it on an intersection, stuffed it with some trash an started the incendiary device. Unfortunately, it was kind of a dud and the fire started to go out. In the distance, we could see the fire truck coming festooned with firemen holding cold beer to put out the fire.

Thinking quickly, perhaps too quickly, I grabbed a can of kerosene and ran toward the outhouse with hope of watching the firemen at work. Just then a car rounded the corner blocking me from my destination.

I was waving them out of the way when the car doors opened and these two guys stepped out, both were somewhere around 6'10" tall and they were wearing 'Smokey Bear' hats. Time once again, for clean underwear. A **Coming of Age** moment for sure.

Can't tell you what they said, but they did cuff me and loaded me in the back seat. I was taken to the main intersection in town, known as Coddy's corner because Harold Caldwell owned the Drug store there. It was easy to find because that intersection had a blinking traffic light. The only one in town.

So there I sat in the back seat of a Highway patrol car wondering if they gave kids the electric chair for Halloween mischief. Even worse, would they take me home to my dad? It might be better if I got the 'Chair'.

Diagonally across the intersection were most of my friends watching to see if I was going to be administered my last rights. There was another problem. The hand cuffs kept falling off.

Years later, I figured it out that I was being used as a scare tactic. Rather effective I would say. Eventually they gave me the option of going straight home or going to Jail. I made a snap decision to go home. I was pretty cool with the guys for some time after that caper.

Today, the out houses are gone. It is probably illegal to have one. Not long ago, I was watching a treasure hunting show on television. The 'Hunters' were looking for locations that previously were the homes for a 'Privy'.They said many 'Treasures' had fallen in there and for obvious reasons, never recovered.

On our farm at Rockdale, Texas, we have the remnants of a Privy in the woods. It should be safe, it has not been used for thirty years at least. It has always been just a few boards in a pile as long as I can remember.

Maybe I should see what I can dig up. With my luck I would probably just find a bunch of crap! That was a really **smelly** joke. Ha Ha

Chapter 13

Greatest Shot Ever

It was my all-time luckiest shot but it was portrayed as pure skill. The one in a million shot that the best trick shot artists would bow down to.

I was a fledgling teenager at the time, always ready for action. One day my dad came home from work and told me his old friend was coming on the weekend to give his new hunting dog a preseason workout. His friend asked if I would go with him knowing full well I would know where the pheasants would be. Let me say right here, this was no ordinary friend of my Dad, this man worked for the Winchester Arms people and was a former demonstration shooter for them. Holy moly, not only did I like him, I worshiped this man.

On several occasions, I had the honor to hunt with him. I would drool staring at his firearms. I just knew that one day he would give me one. Didn't happen!

Saturday morning, I was up about 3 hours before he arrived. When he arrived, he opened the door and his new dog jumped out and quickly started hunting our chickens. A sharp word from him and the dog was quickly sitting at his side.

It was a beautiful Weimararner. It had eyes that could see right through you. This was amazing to me. My best hunting dog, correction, **all** my hunting dogs had questionable ethnic backgrounds. A professionally trained hunting dog like that was WAY out of my league. I was a grown man before I had a hunting dog that had a known family tree.

This man walks up to me to shake my hand. His hand could go around mine twice. I used to go to church every Sunday and sit next to my dad, now here I am shaking hands with God perhaps? Once my feet landed on the ground, God, I mean this man, said he was told that perhaps I could steer him toward some pheasants. You bet. Let's go. He asked if I had a gun and I said sure, it's a .22. That's great he said because he wanted me to shoot over his dog for training purposes.

The hunt begins and I explained there was a bramble patch at the far end of this field. I told him that birds would hold there because beyond the brambles was a creek and the pheasants would not cross it. He said, "Very good young man".

For those reading this that are unfamiliar with a Ring-neck pheasant, they are the Northern equivalent of a Texas Road Runner. I am not sure which I would bet on if there was a race between them.

Half way down the field the dog gets 'Hot' and starts his thing tracking a bird. Then he freezes like stone but only for a couple of seconds. God, sorry, this man says the bird is moving and pretty fast. The dog resumes his Zig Zag pattern in pursuit but the zigs and zags are getting smaller. Right up to the brambles. The dog freezes again, classic pose, one foot still up and he's staring into the prickly shrubs.

The man quietly asks if I could hit a Pheasant with a .22, I said sure. I had shot **AT**, probably a thousand flying Pheasants and I did get one once but I had no witness. He said to come forward on the left of the Dog he would be on the right. Be ready he said. It didn't look like his dog was breathing. WOW.

Next came an explosion of cackling rooster pheasant. So violent was this take off it would give a novice a heart attack. I pulled up, not taking much time to aim, and fired. The pheasant folded like a cheap suit and fell to the ground. The dog bolted on a retrieve like I was his new found friend. I noticed the man was not watching the retrieve but staring at me. I looked at him and he said, "You shot that pheasant"! I said, "You told me to". But, I never thought you could hit it.

The dog brought the dead bird to his master in a very joyful manner. One glance told me I had actually missed my target. The bullet had flown slightly high over the pheasant's back but as luck would have it the bullet caught him right in the back of his head. Instant death. All that remained of the bird's head was some skin and a bill. The man said, "You shot his head off when it was flying". I said "Sure", like it was no big deal. He said, "Don't kill any more". and I said, "Okay".

On the way back to the farmhouse, he told me he would not have suggested the kill if he had thought this farm boy could do it. Dad met us at the barn and my new friend showed him the pheasant and replayed the story in great detail. Dad enhanced the story when his reply to his friend was, **"I am not at all surprised"**.

Sadly, it was in the early nineteen eighties when the man came to Texas to visit my Dad for the last time. They were both in their 80's. One last time I got to hear the story about the Greatest shot he had ever seen. He had the Big **C** and he knew he was going on the Big hunting trip.

Those were REAL Men. I miss them still. Love You Dad.

A post scrip to the previous story. Later that year, the actual pheasant season opened and late in the season he called my Dad to ask if he could come to hunt and that if it was okay, he wanted this farm boy to hunt with him. What an honor. In subsequent years, I hunted with him several times, usually for partridge. Some times I wish I hadn't done that because he quickly learned I was just another bird hunter. That missed birds, especially partridge, a lot.

The real story was that pheasant hunt. I was still too young to hunt legally so I was the guide for him. We had entered this field that had sparse cover for birds yet was usually productive because other hunters would take a look and vote to pass on it.

Not us, part of way through the field the dogs actions made it clear there was more than weeds. ZIG & ZAG there he goes. Tighter and tighter then freeze frame. But only a couple of seconds. Resume the submarine like pattern. On point again. Not for long, he starts to move again but lifts his head looking beyond where I thought the pheasant was. My dad's friend said to just stop and watch what his dog does. Chirp chirp chirp on the dog whistle. His dog started walking backwards about 10 feet. That was a first for me.

The dog then ran to the side of the field and sprinted to the far end then cut back across and resumed the hunt working toward us. All was done with a few 'chirps' on a dog whistle. A few minutes later, the dog turns to granite facing us. My dad's friend said "That bird has nowhere to run" and "that's how it's done young man".

I can still see that episode as clearly as if it happened an hour ago. I sure wish they had Go-Pro back then.

Of note, when I hunted with him his lunch sack always had two Peanut Butter and Jelly sandwiches. One for him and one for his dog, How Cool is that.

I think of you often Mr. Cunningham. You were a good man to hunt with.

A Good Shot

When the boys were getting into hunting and fishing, we spent a lot of time at their grandparent's home at lake Livingston in Texas. It had two things the boys loved. Up the hill and across the highway was the lake. Down the driveway and through the fence, you were in The Sam Houston National Forest. Pretty sweet for the outdoor boys.

On this particular day, Michael and I were hunting together for nothing in particular, just chance opportunities. Jeff as usual was off doing his own hunt. He preferred it that way. I think it was from too much noise and too many questions.

Michael and I are walking along a weed patch, Michael carrying his beloved Ruger 10-22, always ready for the shot of a lifetime. I am carrying my Over & Under 12ga. Broken open and over my shoulder. I had learned a bit about safety through the years. Michael on the left, Dad on the right. Just enjoying the moment. About thirty feet to Michael's left, a swamp rabbit (a cottontail only bigger) breaks cover on a dead run ahead of us. I draw the O/U, close the action, aim and fire. The rabbit tumbles.

Michael acts like I had become a Super Hero. He said we both saw the rabbit at the same time. He was ready, I was not. He said, "You killed that rabbit before I even had my safety off".

He still talks about it today. I guess time just slows down when the action starts.

Chapter 14

Uncle Clarence

My dad was the youngest child in his family. There were a total of nine siblings, seven boys and two girls. They were close all through their lives with one exception. Herman had extricated himself from the family. He went to the extreme of refusing to spell his last name the same as everyone else. Weird ! What was surprising was that his two sons remained close to the family and were frequent visitors to our farm.

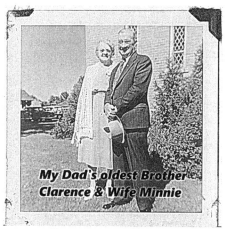

My Dad's oldest Brother
Clarence & Wife Minnie

Now for Clarence. Clarence was the oldest of my fathers' siblings. He was an avid hunter and fisherman. He also had a cottage on Lake Ontario that was close enough to ride my bicycle to. These things quickly jumped him to the top of the list of favorite uncles.

At his primary home in Niagara Falls, he had what today you might call a 'Man Cave'. In the 'Cave' were his gun cabinets with all his guns in view behind glass. There was no need for a safe in those days.

It's a wonder he still liked me, because I would ask questions about every one of those guns. He also had a 'Small game' trophy case with mounts of every kind of bird and small animal I had ever heard of. Lots more questions.. He was a patient man with this kid.

One wall was a big built-in bookcase for magazines. Not just any magazine, National Geographic magazines. He had them all, EVERY issue from day one. I had a few **Coming of Age** moments from those magazines thanks to the native tribes of Africa and South America. I often wonder what happened to those magazines. They must be worth a lot by now.

One of my earliest memories came from my uncle's cabin. Well, I only remember it from home movies that my dad made. There was this little kid maybe three years old walking around drinking from a foamy beer stein. Today, I guess that would be some sort of child endangerment. I still enjoy the taste of a cold brew.

During the summer time, there would be several 'Family Reunions' at the cottage. Not just family, but family friends also. I remember there would be a lot of people at these events. On a sad note, at least for me, was the German language. All prayers and some conversations were in German. My aunts would often ask me if I understood what was being said and I would say yes. The true answer should have been, NIX or NINE!

Maybe when I finish these memoirs, I will start to learn the German language. Better late than never.

After I had learned to drive the tractor, I would load a trailer with the proper implements and drive to the cottage to work his property for his annual garden about two acres in size. I would plow then disc it into submission.

I remember how poor the soil was, mostly clay, the best top soil having been washed away several hundred years before I ever set a plow to it. Still, he managed to grow a lot of melons and Veggies.

A BIG surprise

One day in the summer time, my uncle asked if I would ride my bike down to the lake the next day because there was something important for me to see. The next day, I was there before noon and he said he was going to show me something that few people have ever seen and probably in the near future, would never be seen again.

We started walking toward the lake, several hundred feet away with a bank that was probably thirty feet high. On one side of the property a cut that been dug with a bulldozer that led to his dock. This dock was one of the concrete piers that only extended about ten feet into the lake. That made it just far enough to make it useless to boaters or swimmers.

When we approached the bank, I was instructed get on my hands and knees and be very slow and very quiet. My imagination was out of control. Crawling the last few feet, we slowly peeked over the bank. My Uncle said, "Yep, he's here." I must be blind, I don't see a bear or even a sparrow.

'WHERE?' Right there he said. What? Look at the end of the dock he said. Okay, I see lake water. I think he was ready to throw me over the bank. LOOK IN the water he whispered. Okay, the only thing I could see out of the ordinary was what appeared to to be a sunken log at the end of the pier. I was informed, 'That's no log son'. He said it was a Sturgeon and it was a very big one. What I could see of it, I would say a minimum of six foot long.

I asked if we were going to try to catch it? He said, 'Sure , go ahead.' What with? Use your hands son! He started to laugh then. (Using this kid for humor) .

He told me to remember what I was seeing because he was certain they were nearly extinct. I asked if we could get closer and he said that I could try. I circled around trying to keep it from seeing me. I thought if I could crawl out on that pier, I could peek over the edge and be about three feet from this monster. As I approached the pier my uncle gave me a 'Thumbs Up' indicating he was still there. Moments later, a huge swirl of water and he was off to safety of the deep. As he departed, he actually made a 'Bow Swell' on the surface. He swam way faster than I thought he could. Uncle Clarence thought he must have felt a vibration or heard me.

My aunt Minnie, had a nice lunch made for us and while we ate, my uncle said the Sturgeon would probably be back soon.

I laid at the top of the bank waiting for a long time and a couple hours later, I saw a shadow coming very slowly. The lake was 'Slick smooth', so I could see quite well. Still about fifty yards out, he stopped for the longest time. It appeared there was something not to his liking, because he disappeared back into the deep. I don't think he was ever seen again.

Before I left that day, my uncle showed me a newspaper article with a photo of him and a friend standing with six or so sturgeon that were hanging on a rail. Each fish was as big or bigger than they were. He said they were captured with spears in the Niagara River. Today, they say they are very slowly making a comeback in Lake Ontario. Rest in Peace Uncle Clarence.

My First Shotgun

When I was real young, perhaps too young, I started using a shotgun to hunt. It was my dad's 12 Gauge Model 12 Winchester. It is a heavy gun that was way to big for a kid to handle. I pretty much sucked when it came to wing shooting because of the size and weight of the gun. This grew to be a problem for my dad, because if I could find 20 rounds of his ammo, there would be zero when I came home. What are rounds of ammunition for? My dad would want to go hunting with his friends and there were no shotgun shells anywhere, so off to the hardware store for more.

He did get smarter, come pheasant season, he would give me six shotgun shells. If I didn't get two pheasants with six shells, it was just too bad. That in itself made me a better shot. Things are still that way today.

When my grand kids come to the farm and I have 500 rounds of .22 ammo for them, they will shoot 500 rounds. 1000 rounds? 1000 shots fired, simple math.

The day finally came, I was thirteen or fourteen years old, my Dad said to jump in the car, we were going to Uncle Clarence's cabin. When we got there, my Uncle says he has something he wants me to try out. He went back in the cabin and came out carrying an Ithaca Model 37 featherweight shotgun 12 gauge. I spotted the make and model from 20 feet. I had drooled over them in outdoor magazines for a long time.

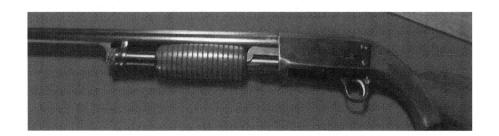

Be still my heart, could it be? I was surely hopeful. It was explained that he was not sure if this gun was any good so he wanted me to test it for him. He had me hold it for examination while he went to his garage. He came back carrying a box of clay pigeons and two boxes of shotgun shells. At this point, I really had to 'suck it up' because my observant eye told be those were not target loads, but they were indeed High Velocity pheasant loads.

Now remember the gun? Featherweight, featherweight = **RECOIL**. So here is this poor kid weighing in at maybe **100** pounds about to do battle with a **fire breathing 12 gauge monster**. My mind is set, **I WILL NOT LOOSE THIS FIGHT!**

I am appropriately dressed in shorts and a T-shirt. Load it up Boy! Oh please, don't PEE yourself. Ready? Sure, Zing there goes a clay pigeon. KABOOM. Clean miss! Holy crap, this thing kicks a lot more than my dad's gun. Let's try another, better lean into it boy. Zing, KABOOM! Busted Pigeon. Yea, I proved myself!

Not hardly, there are still **48** rounds in the boxes. I kept pounding away, breaking more than I missed. It hurt so bad. A couple of times I caught myself crying. This was a **COMING OF AGE** time. Zing, Boom, Zing, Boom, on and on it went. Seemed like they found another couple of boxes of shotgun shells. It never got easier, the last shot was the worst. It was no longer my shoulder that hurt, it was my hair that hurt along with my toe nails and every other part. In my heart, I knew this was my "Man-Hood" test, and, **I WILL NOT FAIL.** (Just make sure they don't see the tears.) Finished at last, Dad says, I guess you can handle it. My Uncle agrees and they said, **it's yours. I slept with it that night.**

Some years later, my uncle told me he brought out two boxes of shotgun shells just to scare me. **It did!** His 'Scare tactic' was quite effective. He said they thought I might handle 5 shots, 10 at the most and then I would 'Beg' off. They just wanted to see if I could do it safely and not fall down after every shot. He said I sure fooled him.

Lasting treasures from my Uncle

Uncle Clarence left me a couple of items from his past when he died. My aunt had a note from him that instructed her to give me a couple of items. One is a folding knife that I always admired from Union Cutlery company in Olean, New York. They have long been out of business. It is quite valuable today.

The second item is priceless. He gave me a matchbox cover that he made during WWI, that's right, **World War One**, while he was in France. It is made from an ammo clip. On one side there is a .45 caliber round that is sliced in half, brass and the bullet. Between that is a french coin. The other side has a .30 caliber bullet split in half with another french coin between the halves.

The top of the 'Clip' is open and that exposes the striker strip on the match box. The bottom is the Prize. It is engraved with two lines. The top line says, "C A Schultz". The bottom line says, "1918 France 1919". How COOL is that?

The matchbox that is with it is from the IRIS match company. The matchbox itself is valuable.

He never would talk about the horror he saw there during the war. I do know that he was sent home after two years because he was wounded. He did tell me how he was wounded because he thought it was funny. He said during a German attack, he dove into his 'Fox Hole' only to find someone else already occupying it. So, Uncle Clarence took one round for his country through both Butt cheeks.

He burst out laughing when he said, "I sure was glad I landed in there face down." I didn't understand that part until sometime after puberty. I said to myself, Now I get it. Ha ha

Thanks Uncle Clarence, you were the Best.

Chapter 15

The Sail Boat

The following story is very short yet in my **'Coming of Age'**, it was huge.

I went to High School in the neighboring town of Wilson N.Y. A pretty cool place that provided many a great memory for me. Wilson was several times bigger than Ransomville and that was rather intimidating at first for this Farm Boy. Wilson is located on the shore of Lake Ontario. They have beautiful summers which make up for the Winter winds that sweep across the Lake from Canada. This is the backdrop for a true **Coming of Age** story.

Ed, a photographer of much significance posts photos of the harbor, sailboats and the jetty piers that protect the harbor from sanding closed. Every time I see one of his fabulous photos, I am reminded of this story. It is about those piers and a sail boat.

My friend Paul and I had gone to Wilson to go fishing. For one dollar, we could rent a rowboat for a whole day. This particular day was perfect. A nice off shore breeze. So we decided to row out to the end of the East pier. It is a long rectangular pier that has interlocking thick steel plates driven into the lake bottom. The interior is filled with concrete. It still stands today.

We rowed out to the end of the pier and then around the far end to begin our fishing. Once tied off there, we were completely hidden from view with the pier being some six feet above the water. After a period of time catching the usual nothing, we could hear the soft jingle-jangle of sailboat rigging coming closer. Soon we could see the top of their rigging. Then the boat appeared. In the front was a man hoisting a sail. Then the rear of the sailboat appeared with a girl and her top was missing.

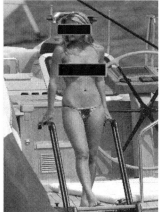

Wow, she was only twenty feet away looking straight at two boys with their mouths wide open. She made a hasty exit to the cabin which was difficult because her hands were busy covering herself the best she could.

Paul asked, "Did you see that"? I said, "You bet I did"! Then I added, "I want to own a sailboat someday"... Paul agreed. I had many dreams about that girl.

P.S. I can't remember if she was pretty, but I do remember a couple of things............

Everyone has a 'Snapshot' of someone or something in their mind that is indelible. This was one for me. **Coming of Age, damn the torpedoes, Full speed ahead !**

Chapter 16

The School Bus

Living in Ransomville and going to high school in Wilson meant there was a long bus ride to be taken twice everyday. I was the first on the bus and the last to get off. I knew where everyone lived. Few knew where I lived. Wilson was only about 5 miles away, but our bus route went pretty much away from school for the first leg of our daily journey. At one point, our bus actually drove around a big rectangle (circle if you will) just to pick up one kid. Being first on the bus did have some advantages. The obvious, my choice of a seat. In the coldest part of winter, the seat right over the rear heater was prime pick. The rear heater was not much, but it was better than nothing.

The other reason was Iva. She was just about the most beautiful girl I had ever seen. One day she got on the bus, walked to the back and sat with me! **She sat with Me!** From that day on, no boy would dare to try and sit with me. It was reserved for Iva. We are still friends today.

Coming home in the evening, my dog 'Wimpy' would be lying in the weeds about a quarter of a mile from the farm near the railroad tracks waiting for my bus. Everyday when he spotted us, he would jump up and run in front of the bus all the way to the farm barking at everyone and everything. Sort of like a Police escort. My bus driver(s) hated him. Both my dog and my bus drivers were upset when I was not on the bus, because I was at ball practice. The escort drill would take place the same as always.

Speaking of bus drivers, we had one that was really a grouch. I guess us kids didn't help. I remember one time Milton the bus driver pulled out from an intersection on a snowy road and gave it a bit too much gas. The rear end of the bus broke traction and began to slide. Milton handled it like a true Pro. He stayed on the gas much to the delight of the Boys and around we went. A perfect 180 with a school bus. I swear it's true. Quite possibly the only slow motion 'spin out' by a school bus, Ever!

On another icy day, Milton Pulled out of an intersection only to find it was already occupied with a car. Neither were traveling very fast, but we 'T-boned' the car. Milton, in true NASCAR style stayed on the gas keeping the car pinned to us. We pushed the car sideways for some distance before Milton noticed something strange in front of us. That driver was rather upset. It was a **'Coming of Age'** moment hearing the words he used to describe our Bus driver.

Brown Bag Lunch

The Brown bag lunch made us all heroes for a time. Well, all but one of us. One spring afternoon we got out of school at the usual time (I think it was 2:30 and the time was somewhat important). Our bus is loaded and with the command of the Vice Principal the buses peel out of the bus parking lot like the well orchestrated affair that it was. The buses would then fan out in all directions. Ours headed South on Town Line road, a long straight road. We didn't drop off the first student until about 4 miles from school.

The bus carried all grades. Grade school kids in front and the very elite high school kids in the rear. Remember the little kids, they are about to come into play.

About three miles into our journey, Milton hits the brakes and pulls off the road. What? He stands up and says, I will never forget this, **"WHO DID IT? WHO THREW THE LUNCH BAG THAT HIT ME IN THE**

HEAD?" Silence... more silence. Milton dips way down into his vast thought process and said, **"We are going to sit here until whoever did it comes forward."** Hmm, must be nearly **3pm**. I see trouble coming here. I am just a High school kid, but I am thinking this is not a good plan. So we sat, no biggie to me, I was sitting with a hottie named Iva. Oh please, make me stay here all night. The siege continues. **4PM** . We're in the back row, Good times! I had a good arm but that throw was beyond my capability. The trajectory would have been comparable to a high powered rifle. Those of us in the back were having a great time.

The clock is ticking. No negotiations. **Way to go Milton! Stand your ground.** We'll worry about grade school kids another day.

About**5pm** , that's right, **5pm** we see a car coming, **FAST**. It goes off the road behind us in a beautiful slide in the dirt and weeds. The door whips open and here comes Clayton, the Vice Principal on a dead run .

Wow, as he runs by the bus, I can see the Veins bulging in his neck. I'm thinking he might be upset about something. He jumps on the bus and asks Milton, with no concern for what the little kids might hear and says, **'What the hell is going on'**? The school switchboard is LIT up with wailing mommies. After being informed of the heinous crime, he told Milton to get us home **NOW!**

At virtually every stop along the route, there was a hysterical mommy wiping away tears. **This is not good!**

The next morning, some of the other students were mumbling about some incident and wanting to know what went down on my bus. We make it to home room and at the appropriate time, the P.A. System starts its customary Hiss, snap, crackle & pop. A voice of supreme authority comes on and says, **"ALL STUDENTS THAT RIDE BUS # 80 IN THE AFTERNOON ARE TO REPORT TO THE AUDITORIUM. NOW!"** I dutifully arise from my seat and head out the door with a swagger and much admiration from a couple of homeroom cuties and proceed to the auditorium. Lots of whispers from other admiring students along the way.

We are instructed to sit in the right section of the auditorium and no talking. Once seated, the curtains open and it is apparent they pulled all the stops for this crime.

There on the stage is Ernie the Principal, next to him is the Sheriff's department and next to him, the Big gun, a **Priest**. WOW this is really big. We are given instructions to come one at a time through the side door to the stage. We will start with **you fellas in the back**.

I think this was the early stages of **Profiling**. **"My Read is, ONE OF YOU IN THE BACK DID IT, GUILTY, PERIOD."**

I was not the first go in, but I was way up there. My turn, I sure hope I did not get framed. I go in and close the door as instructed. They are standing in a semi circle with the **Priest** in the middle.

I am thinking the School Principal was there to administer an immediate beating to the guilty party. The Sheriff was there to charge the culprit with the appropriate law for unlawfully discharging a lunch sack. The Priest was of course there to administer last rights and sentence you to Hell and Eternal damnation. **Heavy stuff** !

But wait, **I'm Lutheran, I can state 95 grievances I have against the Catholic Church.**   Just put your hand on the Bible. Hmm, got me there, it's the same Bible the Lutheran church uses. They thought of everything. Down to business. The principal asks, 'Did you throw the Lunch that hit Milton" ? **NO, I swear on the Bible with Mother Mary as my witness. Maybe I just said No. These dudes were serious.** The Sheriff asks did you see who threw it. Answer **No** ! I was too busy watching a hottie named Iva, not about be watching someone trying to Knock Out Milton.

I was instructed to go out the far door of the stage and to sit on the left side of the auditorium. No talking. I was thinking this will be a real Hoot if a Girl was the Criminal. I was also wondering why they were still holding us. My guess was that if they didn't get a confession, Shock treatments and water boarding was on the horizon. And there we sat, seemed like an hour has passed.

About half way through the detainees, Delton went in and didn't come out! **He did it, I should have known it!** The Bible was too much for Delton. Time passes and then Ernie the Principal comes out and instructs us to go to our assigned classes. Lots of whispers.

Delton did it! I should have figured it, he had a seat half way to the front where he could get a clean shot at Milton. The Brown Bag Caper is **CLOSED!**

Talk about fame. Every kid in school was asking questions and some were actually congratulating me! Delton was no longer in school.

Glen

Then there was Glen . He was a free spirit guy that liked to have fun. He lived just down the road from Iva. We had a new Bus driver then, her name was Mrs. B. Much different than old Milton.

The old school buses had a neat feature, when the door opened, you had two or three steps to climb, then turn left to the seating. There was a nice chrome rail to hold onto while climbing up or down the steps. At the top was a chrome pole that ran from floor to ceiling. I am told this pole is very similar to the poles exotic dancers use. I wouldn't know myself, it's just what I have heard.

Glen had this trick and it was very impressive. When we were coming to his house, he would stay way in the back and as the bus braked for his house he would take off running through the bus, gaining great speed. Just as he would reach the dance pole, the doors would open, he would grab the pole go airborne out the doors for a substantial distance. His feet would never touch anything until he landed some distance away from the bus. I'm telling you, it was a sight to see. If he could do more tricks, I'm sure Ringling Brothers would have signed him.

Like I said Mrs B was different. One day she saw Glen coming on the fly. She opened the doors and then closed them quickly. There was no stopping then. A huge crash and there was Glen, lying in a heap in the stairwell with a broken arm. That would have been the end of Mrs. B. but Glen saved her job when he said he was in too much of a hurry and he slipped.

Another time Mrs. B hit the brakes near the place where the Brown Bag caper happened. This time Mrs. B. demanded the Squirt gun that got her. Finally, Glen got up and went to the front. She said give me the squirt gun. Glen said "Let me off the bus" She said no, thinking Glen was going to hitch hike or something. He told her he knew he was in trouble when she hit the brakes so he threw it out the window. He told her he would go get it for her. She said Go sit down and we drove off. I think that was the end of it.

That was the end of Circus fun on that bus.

Chapter 17

The Sweater Girl

It's true, so here goes. Many times in late High school, I would ride home with my friend Clyde. He was a cool guy that was in the inner circle so to speak. Rather wild, but he was cool. You will hear more about him in other stories.

Clyde drove his Mothers 1952 Chevy and it had a top speed of 82 miles per hour on a flat road. Every where we went, 82 mph, no more, no less. 82 mph.

Paul drove his his Mothers 1954 Chevy and it would top out at 94mph. This was a sore spot for Clyde.

One day we were leaving school and I saw Elma. If you saw Elma, you would remember her also.

Let me put Elma in proper perspective, This was a time in History when NO food products like milk or meats or anything edible had growth hormones or antibiotics. No GMOs, No chemicals period. What I am saying is that if a girl in High School had Big Boobs, she had a lot of something else, she was big everywhere. Big boobs big girl, simple. Now comes Elma, 5'2" maybe. 110 pounds maybe. And she looked better in a sweater than any girl in our school for certain. No Contest. WOW. What a good looking girl. She lived about half way between Wilson and Ransomville so I walked up and asked if she would like a ride home ? She said Okay. Holy Moly !

We get to the car and she just hops in between us and away we go. It's raining steady as we head out of town on Lake road. Lake road runs along Lake Ontario all the way to Youngstown but we would be turning onto Ransomville road, less than half way to Youngstown. We had just cleared the Roosevelt beach bridge when Paul flashes by with a car load of guys making faces at us. The chase is on and as expected Paul is pulling away. It made no sense to me that we were chasing Paul, **WE** had the **THE** hottie with us. Take the long slow route please.

At this point, I might add that Clyde's mother's car did not have the best tires. So here we are tearing along Lake road. Not sure if I can take my eyes off the sweater girl. Getting near Ransomville road. Clyde exclaims with great joy, 'We're catching them'. Umm, maybe because they are turning? UH OH, (It's still raining) Clyde taps the brakes and here we go, a snap 180 and we are going straight down the road backwards at, you guessed it, 82 mph. Rather exciting when you are looking out the rear window going that fast. The sweater girl is sobbing. Another full 360. Still on the road. We should have been in a ditch or on our roof or worse. We are still on the pavement. Amazing. Professional driving skills without a doubt.

Paul, sees us coming and has gunned it to get out of the way. On one of the rotations, I saw some worried faces in Paul's car. Whew, we missed Paul. UH OH, we are going sideways now and we're going to go in the ditch but there is a culvert pipe encased with a big chunk of concrete. Guarding that are two of those triangle concrete posts. We're going to hit. The car rocks to a halt and Clyde asks, how bad is it? I rolled down the window and stuck my head out to look down and see. Both of the posts were within an inch of the car. No Contact.

She is crying now. I am volunteering to comfort her. Paul had stopped up the road and then took off seeing we survived. Elma is **'Coming of Age'** and I was there to help. We got Elma home, she only lived a short way up the road. I wanted to go in to help her calm down, but Clyde demanded we leave because he wanted to make sure the guys in Paul's car would keep quiet. He said his driving was toast if his mom found out.

The sweater girl hops out **without a single word of thanks** for the fun ride and hurries off to the House. It was raining, but she was in the car, how did she get so wet?

Off we go trying to get to town before word gets out. Less than a mile later there is a small hill with a road crossing on the other side. We crest the hill 'Bookin' pretty good. Clyde brakes and here we go again, backwards right through a stop sign. Fortunately, the intersection was clear. Once again we avoided ditches. I know it sure was **not** from skillful driving. Clyde gets out of the car and says, "YOU DRIVE" !

I don't know if Clyde's mom ever found out.

I am **sad** to tell you that **the Sweater Girl never rode with us again.** She missed out on so much fun. What I do know is, Clyde, Elma and myself were **'Coming of Age'** that day.

It Had to Happen

Some time later, we are on the way home and Clyde is driving 50 miles per hour. What ? How will I be able to get my daily adrenaline rush? Clyde says his mother had heard that he was driving way too fast. If she heard that again, no more car for Clyde. We are creeping along at 50 mph. It must be a tremendous strain on the horses under the hood. We are even slowing down to 45 mph for a curve in the road. Seemed strange not hearing the tires crying in pain.

Then it happened. It was like the car said to itself, **"This is not right!"** Boom, clatter crunch! It's a **Classic Oil Pan failure**. Oil and miscellaneous parts are no longer INSIDE the Oil Pan.

The '52 Chevy has blown up !

Clyde says, "**My Mom is not going to believe this.**"

Chapter 18

The Chicken Hatchery

The Chicken Hatchery in Ransomville had to be seen to be believed. A super efficient operation that cranked out baby chicks in a way that would make Henry Ford proud. Do a little research, you will find that at one time, Ransomville's hatchery was the largest in the world. I never knew we had such a claim to fame. People traveled to our little hamlet from as far away as Russia to study and learn how to do it.

There is a historical marker at the hatchery now that talks about it being the largest in the world at one time.

The operation was quite simple, it started with the egg incubator room or did it start with a chicken? The debate continues.

There were a lot of incubators. Each incubator has a lot of eggs. At a prescribed time, one of the incubators would be opened and one rack removed. The rack, about 2' x 2' would be crammed with baby chicks. This rack would be replaced with a rack full of fertile eggs. The incubator itself was like a oblong Ferris wheel. The Ferris wheel was a bit slow, it took 21 days to make a round trip. I think there were about forty egg trays per incubator.

Let's do some math, that would be forty trays times about twenty incubators times how ever many eggs would fit in a tray. That is a LOT of baby chicks.

Okay, we have just removed a tray of chicks. They are carried to the sorting room where without fan-fare, they are swept with the back of an arm into a sorting hamper. The remnants on the tray are dumped into a 55 gal. drum for disposal. The remnants were egg shells of course, unhatched eggs, the occasional dead chick and whatever. The tray was then cleaned and headed for a reload.

Sorting was amazing to me. A couple of people sat sorting the hamper into groups. Roosters and hens, simple. These sorting folks were fast. They would grab a chick from the hamper, turn it up side down with their thumbs between the chicks legs then chunk it into either the Rooster box or the Hen box.

What? I would take one from a box turn it over and examine it carefully, then one from the other box. They were identical to me. The sorters would get a real laugh about my confusion. They would hold up a chick and show me it was a rooster and then show me a hen. Do you understand now? NO! More laughter. I never got it and soon, I had no interest in chicken anatomy.

Knowing that you were smart enough to buy my book, you are probably thinking the hatchery workers must work 24/7. Not so. If a rack of eggs went into an incubator at say 2pm on a Tuesday, that tray was numbered in a ledger with incubator number, tray number, date and time. Twenty one days later on a Tuesday at 2PM that tray was removed loaded with peeping chicks. It's just that easy.

No trays loaded after 3PM, No chicks off after 3PM. Simple. It took a bit of planning when the Holidays were coming, but they worked it perfectly.

The sorting process was important because buyers might want 10 roosters and 50 hens. That's exactly what he would get. A buyer might be only interested in selling cooking chickens, he might want only roosters. And on and on.

This is where I enter the operation. I pestered Mr Rex, the owner until he gave me a job. One day, he finally asked if I could drive a tractor? I stated my vast credentials and he said okay. I was on cloud nine. I didn't even ask about wages. He told me to come the next day after school.

The next day was a long day at school. I arrived at the hatchery and he told me to go get this tractor and trailer and bring it to the rear of the hatchery. I found the tractor but it was way different from the Farmall 'Super A' that was on our farm. This tractor was not the right color either, it was Grey. It's a Ford. My vast resume was with tractors listed only as a Red one, A Farmall Super-A. I was not about to walk back and ask for help so I figured it out myself. I got it running and found the gear pattern after a search through the rubble and dirt. I arrived at the hatchery on this tractor, one happy kid.

Mr. Rex pointed to the 55 gal drums of refuse. He said take them out through the range (where free roam chickens an geese were raised) Then go past the woodlot where you will find a field (maybe one and a half acres) and dump the drums there. He said I would easily recognize it. Then bring the drums back and stack them neatly. Got it Boss. He leaves and I re-position the trailer to make it easy to load. Grab the first drum of Egg shells and it smelled pretty bad, but that was not all. Down in there somewhere there was a chick peeping like mad.

UH OH. I went inside and said there was live chick in there. Too bad was the answer. It was explained that it was no doubt a 'Late' hatch. Meaning it hatched after being dumped in the trash. The operation could not 'Wait' on late arrivals. A **'Coming of Age'** moment for me. SAD ! There was more than one chick alive in there.

The barrels were heavy , but there was no way this boy was going to ask for help. I got them loaded by myself. Off I go sitting like a King on his Chariot. Driving out through the buildings waving to the occasional worker. Just didn't get any better than this. It could however get worse, **A LOT WORSE**. The woods was soon in sight and I continued on. There it is, the dump field without a doubt. The whole field was covered with egg shells in piles three to four feet high.

Now remember at the Hatchery, I said everything went in the waste drums? A slight breeze hit me and I swear the odor was **VISIBLE**. Retch, gag, more retching. Here it comes, can't hold it. Man was I sick. Should I just run? No! I emptied all the drums. Gagging and in tears. IT WAS THAT BAD. This was the second **Coming of Age** moment in one day. I forgot all about peeping chicks.

The thoughts of quitting had declined a bit by the time I got back. Mr. Rex saw me and asked what happened, 'You don't look so good'. Now there's the understatement of the century. He asked how I entered the field? Well, I opened the gate and drove in. He said he was sorry he didn't tell me there were several ways in there and you should always check the wind before entering. A tad late sir (unspoken). The damage had been done, **FOREVER** ! It helped when I found out he was going to pay me $1.00 an hour. I'm going to be rich.

When I got home, my stomach had calmed a bit thanks to a Pepsi Cola that was offered by Mr Rex. My mom was all excited to hear about my first day on the job. My reply was simple, "Mom, do not **ever** fix me another egg!"

Since that tragic day, I have never been able to eat an Egg. I can eat something with egg in it but not the egg by itself. A true **Coming of Age** for this Boy. I was wondering what other challenges I would face in Life.

Chapter 19

Chasing Ducks

Once the Pheasant season ended, it was time to set in motion our plans for an all out defense from the ducks that were invading from the North. It was more like a military counter offensive against the winged attackers.

First came the 'Duck blind' construction. We built many a duck blind. Some were very clever and well hidden. After a few years it became apparent that any disguise was okay. Probably it would be best if your blind looked a lot like a Ocean going oil tanker.

So it came to be the grand duck blind. It was constructed on the end of Tim's pier. He had a cottage on Lake Ontario and the pier extended about ten feet into the lake. This made the pier useless for boats or diving, the water being maybe a foot deep. Almost all home piers were the same way. It's like they got that far when cost and labor to build it hit home and so, that was it. Being made of solid concrete it was however a solid mount for a grand duck blind.

When the construction ended, it was fully enclosed except for the shooting window. A roof to keep you dry was nice. We even had electricity from an extension cord that ran from Tim's cabin. It was BIG. Six shooters across and we were not crowded.

Opening day of duck season that year was highly anticipated. The sun started to rise in the East, decoys out, calm seas. Oh boy here we go.

Soon we saw the first attack coming , it was a lone Merganser skimming the water and turning for attack once he spotted the decoy enemy. Battle Stations ! Ready, ready, the Merganser banks hard left when he realizes it's a trap. Too late, six battle guns roar into action. Eighteen blasts from six guns in about 10 nanoseconds.

There would have been more shots, but the Fed's limited us to three rounds per gun. I always wondered who was lucky enough to get a duck with his fourth or fifth shot?

The lake turned to foam and spray from so much abuse. The spray dropped back into the lake. Hey, we got him! Naturally, somebody quickly said, "I GOT THAT ONE". The arguments began about who got a trash duck that no human would eat.

The floor of our Duck Blind

A system was developed where whoever spotted the invader first, would take the first shot the remaining five guns were there to back up the prime shooter. Other times we just rotated as the prime shooter. This was a great opportunity for serious laughter.

Tim was one of the worst about claiming 'Kills'. We called that one day. Tim excused himself to step out of the blind to send a telegram or something. While he was gone, we UNLOADED his gun and it was replaced as he had left it.

Not long later, here comes another duck on a death mission. The result was the usual roar of gun fire. The duck hit the water and Tim stakes his claim. We laughed so hard we had to have a group 'PEE' to keep from wetting ourselves. Tim, just stared, wondering why his friends had gone crazy. We told him, but he didn't believe us. He swore he shot more than once. It's true.

We tricked him one other time also. This time, he was the first shooter. When the duck came in, he jumped up , pulled the trigger nothing happened except that he flinched so bad he nearly fell out of the duck blind. That duck got away because of a roar of laughter instead of gunfire....

The rest of us had learned, always check your weapon upon returning to your shooting station. Every now and then , you would discover an attempt to get a laugh on you. R.I.P. Tim, thanks for the memories.

The Duck Race

Some times it becomes very clear that you have cheated death. This is a tale of two duck hunters that probably should have drowned or at least been beaten to within an inch of their lives.

The story begins on a very cold late duck season on the Lower Niagara River. For those who are not familiar with the Lower Niagara river, it is the portion of the Niagara river that begins below Niagara Falls and flows due North to Lake Ontario.

It has a lot of water flow all the time. 70% of the fresh water in North America flows through that river. The area where we hunted the elusive ducks was somewhere around one mile wide yet with that much water flow there was always at least ten knots of current. You really appreciate it when you try rowing a boat in heavy current.

There was yet another hazard, the River bank is nearly vertical. A couple hundred feet of that equals danger. Throw in some ice and snow, get the picture? We were kind of crazy. The upside was, we had it all to ourselves, I wonder why?

So on this fine 20 degree day, there is Jim and I sitting in this make shift blind waiting for the kill of a lifetime. Another reason we selected this spot was because we found an old Dory type boat that was still somewhat seaworthy. The biggest problem was one .22 rifle bullet hole in the bottom. A minor inconvenience. Just tip it over each time you beached it. The little fountain in the bottom was kind of interesting.

The hunt begins with the usual barrage of gunfire and watching the birds disappear in the distance. Then it happened, BOOM BOOM BOOM, splash, We got one ! Not just a duck, it was a Greater Scaup, aka Bluebill. To us, this is a trophy.

But wait, we only winged it. Dive Dive Dive ! Just like the German U-Boat movies. We jump up ready to finish him when he surfaces.

Do you know how far a Bluebill can swim underwater? The answer is too far. He surfaces out of range. This is where we should have said, 'We almost had him".

But no, that would not make a story. We need to liven this story up. LAUNCH THE SUB CHASER ! Away we go. All we needed was a kid in the back yelling at us through a little megaphone to row faster.

I wish the duck was just a bit faster so we could turn back, but no, each time he dove we got closer. On and on we went. Finally he dove again a few quick strokes with the paddles and Jim is ready. Surface, Surface. The duck appears and BOOM. We got him.

We only celebrated briefly, because we soon noticed we were closer to Canada than the USA. I think I started hearing Bagpipes playing. Did I mention 10 knots of current? Yep, we are headed for Lake Ontario. Row hard mates.

Then came the bad news, My partner says words you never want to hear, UH OH. What ? I think he was speaking in tongues because I didn't understand him. He was however pointing upriver at a large section of sheet Ice that was on us in a hurry. This Ice flow was a large circle probably a $\frac{1}{4}$ mile across and $\frac{1}{2}$ inch thick. No going around it. Jim busting Ice in the bow, me in the stern paddling like a 25 horsepower outboard. It's sort of working.

Getting near the far side of the ice flow, it seemed to me there was a lot more water in the boat than a .22 bullet hole could provide. I looked toward Jim and quickly mouthed the words **HE** did not want to hear, UH OH! The 'V' in front worked like an Ice breaker. On each side of the bow, there was a slit about 18 inches long and $\frac{1}{2}$ inch wide from the Ice. Plenty of Sunlight and water coming in.

Get in the back Jim !!! The shore is insight ! That boat was now powered with twin Corvette engines. Not sure how, but we made it. Once on shore, we had a long walk back. The temperature had dropped even more. We still had to climb the bank, but that was a pleasure. We could not unload our guns because they were frozen solid. Once in the car and the heater came to life did we start breathing again.

I had been thinking it was strange that we were not seen. Two Fools looking to meet King Neptune. Just as we were entering the Town of Youngstown on the way home, out in the river we see the Coast Guard Cutter speeding up the river. Looking for dead duck hunters I assumed. We just looked at each other and said, UH OH.

Yet another **'Coming of Age'** saga. Easily in the top 5 dumb things, ever.

Chapter 20

More on Ducks

Jim and I located a prime spot on the Lower Niagara River that was quite safe compared to other areas. It was actually in a big cove that had a gentle back current. Ducks loved it. The problem was, at the top of the bank was an Army Post. Fort Niagara on the same grounds as OLD Fort Niagara that was a player in the War of 1812. It had been occupied by the French on two occasions and the English on several other times.

So, we thought we couldn't hunt there, until we met IZZY. He was a tavern owner in Youngstown and like most bar-keeps, he knew **everything**. They were the 1950's equivalent of today's Search Engine. Izzy knew the law and his brother was a lawyer. Izzy told us it was perfectly okay to hunt there as long as we did not set foot above the high water line. If we made that error, we were on the Army Post.

And so the hunting began and it was great. Up river about a half mile was a boat livery/marina. The owner would leave a rowboat out for us and we would pay him after our hunt. What a neat setup. During this time, Field and Stream, aka Eddie, had finished his tour with the Army and he jumped at the chance to hunt with us again. He should have kept on trapping skunks.

The action had started and the shotguns were warming up when Jim leaned over and said, " You know if the M.P.s come, we're not supposed to go up the bank because we would be on the Army post." So? Jim said, "What do we do if they come down the bank?" With that, he motioned with his head up the bank. Yep, two MPs slipping and sliding down the bank.

Come with us they said. We said no way, we are not crossing that line. They informed us that we indeed were going up the bank. The MPs were nice enough to carry our guns and ducks for us.

So we sat in the Provost Marshals office while he was having a nice breakfast somewhere. Eddie was not looking very happy. When the Provost came in, Eddie jumped to attention along with the soldiers there.

I think Eddie was thinking Leavenworth. The Provost goes into this tirade about hunting on Government land and shooting at 4am. Not so, it was pitch dark until 5-5:30. In the end, he let us go and gave us our guns. He said the ducks stay there.

I wish we could have been there when the ducks were cooked. They were all diving ducks that ate minnows and other fish. Cooking one of those ducks was like eating a Mackerel....

The MPs dropped us off and said sorry that their boss was such an Ass.

That afternoon, IZZY gets the word about us. No way he says, I'm calling my brother the lawyer.

That night, Jim called to say Izzy's brother got everything straightened out with the lieutenant that thinks he's a general. Jim says, "Wanna hunt tomorrow?" You bet, I'll call Eddie. Eddie answers and then hangs up on me. No Leavenworth for Eddie.

Dawn breaks the birds are stirring and Jim says those words yet again, UH OH! A look down the shore to the South, There is two uniformed Police coming. Should we run North? Nope. Two more Officers coming from that way. Oh my, Two more coming down the Bank. A hasty water exit? Here comes The Niagara Park Police in their Boat.

Hands up Boys. Just don't shoot. Cuffs etc. what's the deal? The Captain will charge you when we get there. Get where? **Charge us ?** Leave your guns right there and get in the boat.

A quick ride up the river to the Public boat launch where we are introduced to Captain **Musgrave** of the Niagara Parks Police. He begins by demanding which of us had called the Provost Marshal and threatened his Life ! This is not good. I smell a rat and I think it's an Army Lieutenant.

About this time I have been Thinking, **Musgrave, Musgrave, Musgrave,** I know that name from somewhere click on goes the light bulb. My friend Clyde from Lewiston is dating his daughter.

And so, Captain Musgrave let us go after hearing about Izzy, Izzy's brother the lawyer, the duck thief Lieutenant and Clyde. He asked nicely if we would hunt elsewhere. He doesn't want to be called every morning because some **Lieutenant's wife** hears gunfire.

AH HA, Now I get it. We were afraid to go back then because Izzy was some kind of ANGRY ! He probably posted military OFF-LIMITS signs at his tavern.

Eddie refused to hunt ducks with us after that.

Chapter 21

Hunting Mishaps

Over the years, we had a number of, 'Mishaps' that were quite humorous, at least to some of us. There were no significant injuries so I guess you can say they are funny.

The Inflatable Boat

Duck season always had the same problem, we needed a boat. Lake Ontario, where most of our hunting was done, the water is a) deep, b) Cold, c) usually rough. This was bad for us, but great for big water ducks. These ducks flew in flocks anywhere from two to two thousand. The only ducks we had a hope of bringing into shooting range was a lone duck or a small flock up to five ducks. These birds would 'Decoy' because they were looking for a group to fly and feed with.

Without a boat, a decoy set could only be ten to twenty feet from shore. This was difficult for the average duck to see that was passing by at forty miles per hour, flying at an altitude of three feet and was one hundred or more yards off shore. With a boat, a pattern of decoys that worked was something like this.

A smoking pipe configuration.

A concentrated cluster of decoys in front of the blind. (The Pipe Bowl if you will) Outward from the pack about 30 feet would be one or two decoys. Out from that another thirty feet, a lone decoy. Beyond that, another and another forming a line that was curving down wind. (The Pipe stem) The furthest decoy was way out of gun range.

The idea was that a duck might see the furthest decoy and alter his flight plan to investigate. He might then see a second decoy etc. then spot a whole flock of his friends. And so, he had been "decoyed" into gun range.

The problem was the last of the decoys might be in twenty feet of water. I sure was not going to swim in near freezing water. The answer was an inflatable boat. It was pretty big so it was very safe. As I am sure you know by now, we were very 'safety conscious'.

The problem was, It took about half a day to inflate it. Easy solution, leave it inflated. Put it on the roof of Jim's Chevy. No need to tie it off much, just one line off the bow to the hood ornament then roll down the windows and Jim on one side, me on the other side with our arms out the window holding the side ropes of of our barge. It actually worked quite well.

There was no worries about scratching roof paint because anything over ten mph the boat would lift with the airfoil action and never touch the car.

There was a speed limit however. Too fast and the lifting action would begin dragging us out of the car windows. We figured that could be bad.

Many people got a lot of enjoyment seeing these duck hunters passing by on the way to the lake. It was fun. A bit tough when the weather got cold.

Then it happened. Jim for whatever reason, hit the brakes one day. Another **Coming of Age** moment. This one was a lesson about Inertia. The Chevy stopped quickly, the boat said, 'I'm Out of here'. The boat did stop once it was securely impaled on a Chevy hood ornament.

No problem, the boat came with a patch kit. A thorough examination of wound revealed seventy four patch kits would be required. I hear Bag pipes playing and a bugle playing 'Taps' in the distance.

It was all Jim's fault !

86

Scatter Shot

There was one duck blind Jim and I had that was pretty cool. It was mounted in this windfall tree stump so we were actually shooting down somewhat when a duck would decoy.

The problem was it was a bit tricky to get to it. One place in particular was quite steep and on this day, we had some snow. I slipped and slid down the bank , much to the delight of my partner. I did get some snow in my barrel.

Once the decoys were out, I got a small stick and started to make sure my gun was clear of foreign bodies. I then suggested , maybe I should take the barrel off the gun for a more extensive inspection. Jim says, it's fine let's hunt. WARNING WARNING . This advice is from the same guy that killed our boat.

Coming of Age again , err on the side of caution. Here comes the first duck. I spotted him, so I get the first shot. A dumb duck indeed. The duck commits to a straight in approach to land. No escape options. For a duck hunter, this is the shot you dream about. The duck puts the gear down, goes to full flaps.

I stand up and with a roar of the shotgun, the duck banks hard left and leaves. I didn't shoot again, I was so amazed I did not kill that duck. I did however notice that my shot pattern was like thirty feet across at forty feet of distance. What? I turn and look at Jim and he explodes in laughter. What? He can't answer because he's rolling on the floor pointing at the lake. WHAT? Just pointing. I look at the lake again, nothing, but my gun passes and I see it. The last couple of inches of my gun barrel appears to be quite Pregnant.

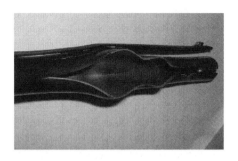

Jim Strikes Again.

The gun above, gets repaired and were off to hunt again. This spot was where we hunted the most. Just off the end of Ransomville road. We could drive a lane right to the lake. Once there, There was a cut of sorts that you could walk down, or drive down.

This was good, the car would be out of sight from the highway.

On this day, Jim parked and we began the unload to carry to the blind. I headed off with the first load. While I was gone, Jim decided to back the car further down the cut. There was one small problem, my shotgun was resting against the rear bumper. I was now the owner of a shotgun that could shoot around most any corner, more great humor for him.

That WAS his Fault !

Chapter 22
The Deer Hunt Shootout

In our later Teen years, Charlie opened a gun shop in town and for some strange reason he took a liking to Jim and I . Paul was off to the Marine Corps so he missed out on this one. Jim and I were asked to shoot on their skeet team, not because we were great shooters but because we would carry a high handicap. Then as we improved, our team would move up the ranks. I was amazed how much better a shooter that made me.

For a time, I worked part time watching the store so Charlie could do whatever. During that time in the store when it was not busy, I would reload shot shells for the skeet team plus more for me. Every box I loaded for myself would cost me 50cents.

That covered the primers, powder, wads and the shot. The price tells you how old I am...

Okay, the Deer Hunt. Charlie asked if we, Jim and I, would like to make a Day trip with him to hunt the Southern Tier region of New York? Great, we would leave at 4am on Saturday.

Jim told me his parents were gone to see Paul, for a few days in North Carolina, who was in the Marine Corps, so why didn't I come to spend the night?

Friday I get all my gear together and go to Jim's house. Too boring watching TV and too wound up thinking about a monster buck waiting for us. Let's go have a beer.

The Porter Hotel had the welcome mat out for us. There were only two "establishments" in town, the other being Johnston's restaurant. We were not welcome there because the owner was Jim's uncle and Jim lived there when we first met. Harold, the owner, told us to NEVER come in there to drink beer and we knew he meant it.

So, the Porter hotel it was. Get the 5 Star nonsense out of your head. I'm thinking maybe 1/8 of a star. You know, I can't ever remember seeing a paying guest. So we wet our whistle with an ice cold Genesee beer. Trivia, Genesee Bottling Company is the oldest operating brewery in the United States. You just thought it would be in Milwaukee. Google that.

Well we decided to have another and at 2am we were evicted. The beer and the stories were amazing. Somehow, we got back to Jim's house. It was only a long block away , About ¼ mile. No one stepped on our fingers either. Too late to sleep now so we head for the basement.

His parent's house was one of those 'Ranch Style' homes with one level that was long. The stair well came down at the South end and at the North end, there was a wood box with a target on the front.

I am sure you are now thinking, oh no, guns and Alcohol.

You may not want your kids to read beyond this point.

It started safe enough, but how many .22 rounds can you shoot at a target before it gets boring. In our case, not many. But wait, here's a great idea, lets take this light bulb, hang it from the floor joists above and swing it in front of the target. Not only aim straight, but you had to have timing..... Our timing sucked. Much laughter. Jim was sitting on the stairs fumbling around trying to reload a tube fed .22.

I eased over to his gun rack and deftly lifted a model 1897 Winchester pump shotgun, slipped in a #6 Pheasant load and that 12 gauge was ready to talk dirty!

My timing was spot on. With a roar and a flash that was **way** beyond your imagination the light bulb vanished. I wish you could have seen Jim's eyes. They looked like two white Poker Chips. We didn't communicate too well due to the loud ringing in our ears. Man that was loud ! The laughter started. I was laying on the steps holding my rib cage and wondering if the light bulb had come to rest as yet.

A good time to look away now.

About that time, there was a second equally loud explosion and I was **HIT**. Right in my left cheek. It hurt! I grabbed my face knowing half of it was gone. Prying my hands away was scary, thinking my face would fall off, but it revealed only a large red welt under my left eye. No blood. Talk about instant Sober !

Next, Jim said, how could it have hit you? I know I was pointing away from you.

Oh No ! Where DID it go? What do you mean by that? He said, It was a **12 gauge Rifled Deer slug.**

Yikes , that's like $\frac{1}{4}$ pound of solid lead. The search begins , how hard will it be to find a 1" hole. We checked all the concrete walls, nothing. Crap, we really didn't want to go upstairs. That round would go up through the floor then a wall, then the ceiling, out the Roof and possibly take down the neighbors mighty Oak. Get the picture?   Nothing upstairs either. What?

Back to the Basement. We are sitting on the steps doing a rewind an Jim says, "OH NOOOOO"! I looked and he is pointing down the basement. I do not see a thing. He says,"RIGHT THERE!" still pointing.

Remember I said this was one of those long Ranch style homes? This style home has a center structure beam that runs its entire length. It in turn is supported by steel pipes that are embedded in the concrete floor. The first of the support pipes had been "Center Punched" by a 12 ga. rifled slug, not 10 feet from where I sat.

There was a hole the size of a fifty cent piece on one side and a chicken egg size bulge on the other. These are heavy gauge pipes. So, mystery solved, it was shrapnel that hit me.

Coming of Age? You Bet.

No need to worry about that now, our ride is here........Let's go hunting.

Jim would never admit it, but I am pretty certain we both had a good nap in the woods that day.

Later, the chicken egg was beat back in somewhat and the Hole filled in a like manner. A quick splash of paint and it was awful, the worst body and fender repair I had ever seen. It actually worked for a short period of time until one day his dad went down to the basement. A few minutes later , there was a Thunderous 'God Damn It' !

I knew it was time for me to go home.....

Chapter 23

The Slo Pokes

When I was an early teen, the guys from Ransomville that were a little older than me formed a car club called the Ransomville Slo Pokes. Not for Hot Rods, but for Stock car racing. Make no mistake, these guys all had fast street cars also.

Their first track was a small 'paper clip' shaped track that was located behind Ed's garage. The track itself was so rough, Roll-overs were common without ever being touched by another car.

Ed's garage at one time was a Kaiser Frazer dealership. Since then, it was simply Ed's garage.

The early days were really simple, spectators were few, so they could drive out behind the garage and through a field , then sit in your car and watch the Jalopy races. During intermission, the drivers would walk through the few patrons with a helmet taking donations.

Nearly all the stock-cars were built in Ed's garage. A lot of us kids worshiped those guys. I would spend hours watching them building their cars and talking of racing. NASCAR was still a few years off.

One of the drivers, Ed, as in Ed's garage was truly a gifted driver. He teamed up with John, an engineer who also had a stock car but was not nearly as gifted a driver. So it became John the engine and car builder with Ed the driver. Brains and Guts if you will.

Year by year it grew. Soon, a Piece of property was purchased, a real racetrack built and Ransomville Speedway was born. Then the racing had expanded to Merritville, Ontario. Friday Ransomville, Saturday Canada.

Peter and I got into the action when we got old enough and built a

1955 Chevy late model. We never did very good. We won a few heat races but that did not cover expenses. In stock car racing, no sponsors equals poor equipment. Simple. Pretty much every dime I earned went into racing.

That was a fun time.....

Ed and John

When NASCAR started up, things were pretty testy. You had to be a NASCAR member to race at a NASCAR track. If they found that you were racing at 'non sanctioned' tracks , you were banned from all of their tracks. Drivers were racing with fake names etc.

With the advent of NASCAR, came RULES. To give you an example of how clever John was, there was a rule that said in the Modified Sportsman Division, you could not have a car with the engine setback. A car that had the engine setback a foot would be a superior balanced car and was a dream to set up for cornering. The set back was prevented by the X member frame.

The actual rule stated the rear of the transmission had to be mounted in the center of the X. Simple rule check, is that engine set back? Crawl under the car and look. No, the transmission is right where it's supposed to be. Perfectly legal.

John says, time to build a new car with a setback engine. What? Quite simple really but he was the only one in NASCAR to think of it. The front axle and suspension was moved forward and the rear axle and suspension moved forward also. The body was modified so the fenders were again over the wheels. A strange looking car for sure. A look from the side said something is not right. A lot of races were won with that car. This is true, I helped build that car.

Hmm, How did that engine get way back there?

The following year, NASCAR changed the rule book to stop that.
The Drivers

I saw many great drivers come through our area. Richie Evans for one. He is in the NASCAR Hall of Fame.

Richie Evans

The Treichlers, Merv and Roger were Modified Sportsman National champions.

Roger and Merv Treichler were my next door neighbors before my family moved to Ransomville.

To me, the best was Ed, Driving car #0. In his era, NASCAR starting lineups were inverted, meaning the car with the most points started last. I can still hear the speakers as they announced the lineup. It was always the same, "and the car starting last is ZERO". I had heard the final count of his career was 199 Feature wins. He was the best I had seen.

My grandson asked who was the greatest driver ever? I told him we would never know, because the greatest driver ever probably could not find sponsors to help him get started. Who knows, it might have been me. Ha Ha

I lived for my fast cars. Doubt it? Just ask the girls that left me because of my cars. At one time, I owned three '55 Chevys . My street car, my stock car and a third for parts.

Chapter 24

Lewiston Pacers

The 'Hot Rod' days of our late teenage years were action packed for sure. Several of us started hanging around with some guys from Lewiston. I can't remember how it started. I think it might have been because of the 'Burger Basket'. That's where the Hot Cars were and the pretty girls showed up there also. Normally guys from other towns were rejected without a trial. For some reason, we were accepted as hot rod guys, not a gang from out of town.

There were three of us that hung out there primarily. Kenny, myself and Clyde from Ransomville. (For the rest of this story, Clyde from Ransomville will be referred to as Clyde ®. You will soon understand. (I sure hope I don't miss anyone here,) The Cast of characters from Lewiston were Clyde (L), Floyd, Bill, Joe, Tom and Tim. They were unique characters that I will not describe here.

We had many good times together. Lots of laughs and beers. The biggest arguments were over Cars. Mostly who's was fastest. Tim was the winner there. His '57 Chevy with a factory 270HP engine with two Four barrel carbs, was WICKED fast. He won most of the time at drag races.

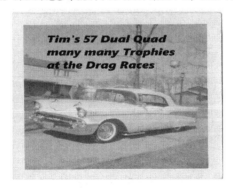

Tim's 57 Dual Quad many many Trophies at the Drag Races

The Cars, Clyde ® '55 Chevy, Clyde (L) '55 T' bird , Floyd '57 T' bird, Bill '52 Olds, Joe '56 Ford, Kenny '55 Chevy, Tom '55 Chevy, Myself '55 Chevy, and Tim with the '57 Chevy.

The Lewiston Pacers were formed. No Constitution, no by-laws, no treasury, no nothing. I guess Clyde (L) was president. The closest we came to building a Hot Rod was a 1931 Ford Model A pickup. Clyde (L) and I owned it, but Uncle Sam ended that. Those damn Draft Cards.

There was much rivalry within the club the biggest of those were between Kenny and Tim. Kenny was determined to beat him one day. So much so, that Kenny had a well known engine builder build him a 'Big Block' motor topped off with Six (that's right, 6) Carbs and it got stuffed into his '55 Chevy. Quite a task. The problem was, it was not Fast. So the big race-off, never happened. Neither of them were willing to take a chance of losing a race. Funny.

Tom loved his Chevy and always thought it was way faster than it was. When you rode with him and he took off fast (Like there maybe was one slow take off, ever)

He would grab second gear and throw himself back in the seat like there were some tremendous G-Forces involved. We soon caught on and so if you were riding with him, you would simply lean forward with his Power shift, indicating there was negative G-Forces. He found that to be very irritating.

In 1959 and 1960 we were at the NHRA National Championships in Detroit. A car from the 'Ramchargers' club in Detroit came tearing down the track and at mid point of the track, they blew a clutch and flywheel that caused a lot of damage, including severing both the fuel and brake lines. A tremendous fireball followed and there was no hope of stopping the car. Right in front of us, something fell off the car. That something was the driver, an engineer from The Chrysler Corp. He was on fire just like the car. He tumbled down the track for a considerable distance. When he stopped, he managed to get up, but he was still on fire. His flames were put out with a fire extinguisher. He died some time later. The car went down this big ditch that was there to protect spectators. It burned to nothing.

I tell you the above because Tom was there and saw what I had seen. We were unanimous in our conclusion that if the driver would have jumped a lot earlier than he did, he probably would have suffered one awful road rash, but we were certain he would have lived.

Back from Detroit, Tom is driving down the road with a friend when the tygon tubing feeding his three carbs leaks, catches fire then erupts. Flames burst through the boot that seals the steering column to the 'FIRE' wall. Without hesitation, Tom is gone. His friend in the Passenger seat looks for some help from Tom, But Tom is long gone.

His friend reaches over and steers the HOT rod through an apple orchard, then runs when the car is nearly stopped. Tom lost a lot of forearm skin on that one.

My Biggest Win

We had seen advertisements about the IHRA having regional championships for all classes at Erie Pa. At that time, there was the IHRA and NHRA. The 'I', meaning International. The Pacers fielded three cars, Myself, Clyde (L) and Tim. There was a large crowd so probably not much chance for a win.

When we got there, Tim looks around and there is a car that had beaten him before. He says, I'm out of here and leaves to get to another Drag Strip that is holding a regular event. A couple of chicken comments and he leaves.

It's Race time, Clyde is cruising along in his division winning races one at a time. I'm doing good also. The word has it that the winner of each class will have to go through inspection. Nothing strange about that.

Time for the finals. Clyde edges another car by about an inch for the win. WOO HOO.

Finally it's my turn. The flag goes and my car is running strong but this guy is pulling ahead. The race is over quickly and I knew it. We turn off at the end and I was instructed to follow the guy that beat me to the inspection area. So I follow his '56 Chevy (56 is important) to the inspection area.

We were not allowed to touch our cars. They pull him in for inspection and open the hood. I look in and right away, I see he has a really clean engine. Instant suspicion.

They open the distributor and say okay.. Then they pull a valve cover. Start it up. Sure sounds rough, They ask if there is a race cam. NO. he says, but being a Chevy guy, I can see he has double valve springs. Never before seen on a '56 Chevy.

That is not the issue, the race officials determine he has solid lifters in his engine. '56 Chevy's and later had Hydraulic Lifters. Sorry sir, you are disqualified.

My turn , they open the distributor and say okay. Pull a valve cover. I ask if they are checking for Solid lifters? Inspector says Yes. I mention that '55 Chevy's had solid lifters from the factory. A couple of other officials agreed and they said, Congratulations. A Photographer came and took my photo by my car.

At the awards portion , I got a Trophy nearly 3 feet tall (normal Drag racing trophy was about 6") a Bond and a Jacket that said, " IHRA Presque Isle Timing Association Regional Champion".

The Winner

I still have that Trophy. I think the jacket left with an ex-girlfriend. Not sure about the Bond.

Clyde (L) and I went home the big winners. We never did get a straight answer from Tim about his day.

Gone

Clyde (L) is gone now. On his way home from California, he was killed in a Head-on collision.

Kenny was killed in an auto accident with a bridge.

Tom was a Cancer victim.

When Clyde was killed, we had a Club party in his honor. I can't remember a better party.

Chapter 25

The Cottage

My friend Clyde's parents owned a small cabin on Lake Ontario. The cabin was not much, a couple small bedrooms and a living area. I don't think anyone ever slept there. Over the years, the cabin crept closer and closer to toppling over the bank edge to oblivion. Who could sleep without a 'Falling' nightmare?

Even so, it was a cool place for us kids to hang out. We spent hours learning hand eye coordination using a piece of driftwood for a bat and beach stones for a ball. Blasting those stones with a driftwood bat was fun. We knew we were headed for the Major Leagues.

As we grew older, the games became more serious. There was a time I remember one of the gang showed up with a pipe cannon. I think it was Clyde. He was pretty clever with things like that. It was a simple device, maybe a foot long piece of 1 inch pipe. One end was open and the other end was threaded with a threaded cap on it. Just above the cap was a fuse hole that had been drilled.

A powder charge was inside that had been made by disassembling numerous shotgun shells. It was the propellant that was available. None of that wimpy black powder. A steel ball bearing that neatly fit in the cannon bore should be adequate to sink one of those freighters steaming by about five miles off shore. The fuse was equally simple. A soda straw wrapper with a small amount of gun powder in the business end. The remainder of the fuse was twisted tightly. When lit and then blown out, the wrapper would slowly smolder until it reached the propellant charge.

Launch Day

Perfect! No wind, the lake like glass. At the top of the bank, a small trench was dug that held the canon nicely pointed up about 45 degrees to get maximum range.

Ready? Light the fuse and it is smoldering perfectly. Take cover ! We all ran to the far end of the cottage and nobody wanted to peek. We waited and waited. Nothing. Wait some more. Nothing. Better check the fuse. Not me. Wait some more. Nothing. Seems like a half hour passed. Surely it's gone out. Voting on what to do is underway....... Then

KABOOM

The loudest noise I had ever heard. The dust and dirt clears. Where did it go? Way out there, we see a geyser of water. Holy Moly. Check the cannon. It's gone. The launch pad trench is four times bigger than it was. No cannon, just a hole. We decided it was best to head for home.

Parking Area

Later in life we got into cars and girls. The cottage was still a big part of our lives. What a great place to take your girlfriend to do what ever she might be in the mood for. You know, submarine races etc.

Winter Time

With the cottage located on the South side of Lake Ontario there were no distractions or lights to obstruct the view of the Northern Lights in the winter coming from the North Pole. Very romantic for the girlfriends.

During the peak of winter in Ransomville, January and February, it got bitter cold. Outdoor fun was restricted. The cottage to the rescue.

We would park a car parallel to the bank. Then we would shoot at ducks flying by with .22 rifles. One shooter in the back seat, one in the front. The car heater on full blast. That is a perfect duck blind.

Big water ducks fly fast right along the surface of the water. Easy to see where the bullets hit. Several thousand rounds fired, zero hits. Nothing boring about that.

Chapter 26
The Walleye

In the beginning of my story, I said I would only write about "Fun" times. I have been debating with myself about the story that follows. I have decided to tell it before I am gone. I was an 'Eye Witness' to these events.

I was lucky enough to get to fish on the Niagara River before it became too polluted to sustain life. We would drift fish the lower Niagara for Blue Pike and Yellow Pike, known to the rest of the world as Walleye. They are making a slow comeback today, but nothing like yesteryear.

Fishing with my uncle Clarence, my dad and my cousin Sonny, the days catch was not numbered in fish, but in baskets filled. When you found the right drift, action was non-stop.

Then came the chemicals. Most of the chemical factories had little or no waste treatment facilities. Waste and spills simply went straight into the Niagara river. Out of sight, out of mind you see.

The Love Canal

Sudoku

Going Easy On You...

		3			7			
	7				3	6	5	2
	4		1		6			9
9		6					7	
		7			9			
	2				8			5
2			6		1		9	
7	9	4	5				8	
			4		3			

Knuckle-Cracker

5					8	7		
	3		2					
6					4	9		
	7		4			6		8
	4						7	
1		6		9		2		
	8	7						5
				3		6		
	1	6						4

Brain-Buster

				9	4		6	
	6	1		9				
3				7	8			
			2		3		8	
2								1
6		5		4				
		1	4					3
		2		8	7			
4			7	5				

Mind-Numbing Frustration

				5				8
	9		2				1	7
		1						4
			4			7		
2	1					9	5	
	8		3					
3				8				
7	1			9		6		
9			4					

world's last naturally-occurring population of Whooping Cranes on their wintering grounds. Additional festival activities include birding and nature boat and bus tours, interactive workshops and seminars, a painting and wine tasting class, and a free nature-related trade show.

Port A is famous for nightlife and endless varieties of food, entertainment and great shopping. Accommodations for all lifestyles and budgets include hotels, vacation homes, condos, cottages, and RV parks.

"Big Bloom" Plant Sale at the Botanical Gardens April 7

The "fix is in" for the August hurricane, December snow, and hard winter freezes! South Texas Botanical Gardens & Nature Center's annual BIG BLOOM mega Plant Sale, garden festival, and Dollar Day, will be 9 am to 5 pm, Saturday, April 7, on Gardens & Nature Center grounds, 8545 S. Staples St. Visitors may shop and tour the entire Botanical Gardens for just $1 each. Members are admitted free, and may begin shopping at 8 a.m. Parking is free with festival entrance through Rose Pavilion. More than 6000 attended BIG BLOOM 2017!

wetland boardwalk. Food trucks will be on site for lunch! Corporate sponsors u n d e r w r i t i n g DOLLAR DAY include Bay, Ltd., City of Corpus Christi Solid Waste Services, City of Corpus Christi Water Utilities, Jason's Deli, Port Corpus Christi, Valero Energy Foundation, RICOH.

Shoppers are asked to bring plant carriers. Vendor spaces available through April 4. Visit stxbot.org; call 361.852.2100.

Plant include the popular orchid sale, sponsored by Corpus Christi Area Garden Council; plumeria; water-conserving native, Xeriscape and lots of other durable landscape choices, tropicals and exotics; roses, butterfly attractor plants, herbs, tomatoes, peppers and more. Independent vendors will offer more plants plus outdoor décor and other nature and garden related...

This was a canal that supplied water from the upper Niagara River (the river above Niagara Falls) to water turbines below Niagara Falls. When that power generating facility shutdown, being obsolete, a canyon was left right through the city of Niagara Falls. What to do with that? A land fill naturally. The chemical industries had plenty of things to get rid of. Simple, just dump it all in the canal. Later, smooth some dirt over it and sell lots.

All's well until people living over the canal started dropping dead. A lot of terrible toxins were found. The Federal Government bought all the houses. They say the area has since been "Cleaned". If you want to believe that, I have a challenge for you. Go to the Devils' Hole State Park, hike down to the rivers edge below Niagara Falls, then upstream about a quarter of a mile. You will find a cave there. The challenge is to go in the cave and remain there for 2 minutes without choking on chemical fumes that are leeching out of the rock layers. It is disgusting.

Goodies

Later in life, I got a job working at a plant that was to make a 'Special' fuel for the 'B-70' Bomber. It was supposed to be the Ultimate Bomber for the U.S. Air Force. This was an exotic fuel that was hypergolic, meaning that no ignition source was required. It would ignite when exposed to air. Big Problem! Take a cap off a bottle of it and you had a fire. Nasty.

The worst part was the fumes. Breathe it and you got sick, sort of like being super drunk. It was called "The Goodies". We were never told what the chemical was that caused this. Each time a worker was exposed to the 'Goodies', the longer the effects lasted. Nasty! Some of the worst cases came from employees that worked at the 'Burn Pit' a waste disposal area. I remember seeing some of those guys walking the sidewalk going to medical. It was not pretty.

The Burn Pit was a real masterpiece of engineering. It looked like a small swimming pool but with no concrete. Just a rectangular hole dug with a bulldozer. Simple. Just dump the chemicals in the pit, ignite it with a blasting cap. What about all the chemicals that soaked into the soil?

There was another problem, waste from the laboratory. The left over samples were pumped into cylinders like a welder would have for his cutting torch. Now what? They were hauled to the 'Burn pit', lined up along the back of the pit. Then a couple of borrowed soldiers from the

Military storage area, would shoot the cylinders with AP (armor piercing) rounds. It was quite spectacular. No ignition source required. The fuel burned brilliant green. Sound crazy? It's what I saw.

How far would the ground water spread the contaminates? Would you like to drink from my well?

There was another problem, One portion of the manufacturing had a waste product called 'Yellow Solids'. What is it? None of your business! This waste was also hypergolic. Simple, just put it in 55 gallon drums and then fill the drum with Carbon-tetra chloride. A chemical that was used in fire extinguishers until it was found to be a carcinogen. NICE! What to do with the drums? We'll worry about that later seemed to be the strategy.

The drums were placed in rows in the remote areas of the compound in 20 foot intervals. Why? The drums started to bulge. Things are active in there. My friend Clyde and I got a work assignment one day to take a load of these drums to a place called 'NECCO' park, a waste disposal area in the city. Not far from Love Canal. Pretty scary I can say.

We got the drums to the disposal area without any explosions. How to unload this stuff. Simple, remove the rear gates from the truck, back up as fast as the truck would go, slam on the brakes, Grab 1st gear and floor it. Instant inertia off-load. Just don't look back. That stuff is still buried there.

The B-70 Bomber

Without a doubt, the best thing that ever happened to me was when the Government shut down the B-70 Bomber project. No aircraft equaled no need for this exotic fuel, and so the facility shut down.

I remember Bell Aero Systems took a cylinder of this fuel to another portion of the compound where they were testing rocket engines. I think it was for the development of future space craft. Engine start in 5-4-3-2-1, Ignition and the test site was obliterated. They decided the fuel was a bit too much.

After Uncle Sam had extracted his pound of flesh from me, I was hired by duPont and I was happy to be there. There were environmental issues there also. Bisecting the plant was Gill Creek that emptied into the Niagara river which ran parallel to the plant. Nothing lived in Gill creek, **nothing** , not even algae. The Workers called it 'Acid Creek' and the saying was if you fell in , they would pull out a skeleton. Nice.

Because of weather concerns (winter) most of the processes were enclosed in buildings. Most buildings had a 'French' drain running down the center of the building. The floors would slope toward the drain. Any chemical spill would go to the drain and then be washed straight to the river.

Next, I was transferred by the company to Texas. Huge change in attitude about pollution. It made me really think about what I had seen and DONE.

The Great Lakes and the Niagara River have improved dramatically since I left for Texas. Water clarity and wildlife are continuing to return. It is a good thing.

Chapter 27

USAF The Beginning

Like everyone my age, I carried a 'Draft Card'. The general classification on a card was 1A, meaning you were in the Prime grouping to be drafted. While I was going to Erie County Tech, my classification was 2S, meaning we would be in an all out war before I would be 'Drafted'.

When school ended, I went back to 1A. It was just a matter of time. My time was up when I was invited to partake in a draft physical. They found I had two arms and two legs. Passed!

My thoughts of being an infantry soldier was not very appealing. I had family that served with honor during WWII in the Air Corps. A cousin was a B-17 Pilot.

Time is running out and I decided to talk to the Air Force people. Lots of testing. They said I could choose any school that had openings in the Electronics or Mechanical areas. Looking over the opportunities, I spot it, 'Missile engine Technician for the Atlas 'F' ICBM'. WOW, Cape Canaveral, John Glenn, the American Way and being a Patriot. Sign me up!

It was not long before I discovered they did not let enlisted Airmen anywhere near a missile that an Astronaut would ride. No, the reality was that this farm boy became a groundhog, spending all of his time underground doing trivial work on a missile that just sat there 24/7. Boring!

I realized early on that my decision process was not the best in the world. My first day was August the tenth. August! Herded onto a plane in Buffalo, off to Chicago to meet more 'Heroes'.Then we were loaded on a TWA Constellation. The biggest aircraft I had ever seen. I decided that it was nothing more than an aluminum sausage that was stuffed with humans. The big shock was stepping off that aircraft in San Antonio Texas in

August. UH OH ! This is HOT and it is like 1am. Yikes. So it's off to do paper work, get group assignments etc.

They then herded 50 of us outside to meet our leader, he's like 6'6" tall and he is Solid. He has Grey eyes that look straight into your Soul. He is standing there very stiff with his arms behind his back. He says, "Line up in four rows, just like corn in a field". He politely asks if anyone has any objection to him using foul language from time to time. (Sure, like some idiot is going to put up his hand) Hearing no objections, he let us know we were the lowest form of humanity that existed, using very eloquent juicy words.

The First Discipline

We were ordered off sort of mob fashion to a mess hall for breakfast, somewhere around 3 or 4am. Outside the mess hall. A number of flights marched by very military like popping their heels into the pavement as they went by. Some of them called us 'Rainbows' as they marched by. Later, I found out that a 'Rainbow' was a recruit that had a multi-colored uniform. That was us, no military war suits yet.

That same time frame, Grey Eyes says, "When you enter the Mess Hall, you will take only what you can eat, You WILL eat all that you take. Is that understood?" Yes Sir. WHAT? YES SIR !!!! The food was pretty good. I was starved by then.

It had to happen, some poor kid at another table says something about not feeling good and he can't eat.

We had been instructed to stay at our table until everyone is finished. UH OH, Grey Eyes hears or senses a problem. Here he comes. What's going on here? I can't eat sir, I don't feel good. **WHAT? YELLING NOW,** Grey Eyes says, **I TOLD YOU TO TAKE ONLY WHAT YOU YOU COULD EAT!** Several other bad ass instructors join in. That food is government property, you took it, you **WILL** eat it. They helped him eat, **all of it.**

I will spare you the rest of that story, except that the recruit also had to clean up the mess he made. We were made to watch. And so the first major lesson about taking orders and what Rank means.

Oh boy, Let's get our shots

The day arrives we all were dreading, shots, lots of them. John lived in the bunk above me and marched in the formation behind me. He said he was not good with needles and asked me if I would switch positions with him and then I would be in position to catch him if he was going down. Umm, Okay.

We get to the building know affectionately as 'The Green Monster'. This is where everything happens. Hair cuts, clean underwear, dentists, just everything. Get in line to go in and John deftly slips by me without being seen. Inside, I see they are dispensing shots at an alarming rate.

Something new, the shots are being blasted from guns. I had seen this new development on the news. Yea, no needles. Our turn, John steps forward and whack, one blast in each arm. He's going down, I catch him and whack, whack, I get one in each arm. Hey, that hurt. John takes two more for God and Country. He has turned to Jello. Two more for me. Not fun, my muscles were tight from holding John. On we went.

John was not any help when I drug him out the other side of the building. I noticed I had a blood trail on one arm. We are forming up to move out and John is becoming somewhat coherent again. He switches positions with me and says, "That wasn't so bad". He thought he got two shots.

So it was that the "Guns" are for speed, not for comfort. We switched places every time there was a medical procedure. The last time we went for a shot was to get a Polio booster. Simple, one and done. John did great, no assistance required. We are out side and had not been able to switch back when I noticed it was getting dark. I'm on the way out. John turns around and there I am sitting on the road with my head between my knees.

Basic Training Funnies

The Pith Helmet

There actually was some funny things that happened. The first was Pith Helmets. It was so Hot in San Antonio, we were issued Pith Helmets like you might wear on Safari. Here are 50 guys marching everywhere with their Bright White helmets.

Almost as soon as we got them, we were marching somewhere and one of the troops made a misstep. Grey Eyes disappears then here he comes up through the formation until he is behind the soldier of not so good fortune. He raises his clipboard over his head and with both hands, caves in the helmet of the miss-stepper. The helmet is not so pretty now. It is all crumpled and when pushed back into shape it had all these brown spider web cracks. This routine continued for the next few weeks. For a while, I was thinking this was a contest and at the end of Basic training, the last remaining intact helmet was going to win a prize. It got down to about ten or so perfect helmets.

Mine was one. of them. I had a revelation one night, that there would be no prize for a perfect Helmet. It was not difficult to see that Grey Eyes was watching the good helmet boys very closely. The revelation was , **HE'S GOING TO GET EVERYONE!** That night, I went behind my bunk and caved in my helmet on my buddy's foot locker. He asked what I was doing. I said I would tell him later. I was right, I was the only one that did not suffer the 'Clipboard Crunch'

Light 'em Up.

We had been training for 5 weeks and one day we were on the drill pad and we drilled for quite a while without a single error. Grey Eyes gave the order to halt and said we had done really good. So he said, "Rest, LIGHT 'Em UP." and he proceeded to pull out a pack of smokes and light one. He had a couple of puffs and he heard some mumbling.

He looked up and said, "What, 50 guys and there are no smokers?" Louder mumbles. During that time virtually everyone smoked. He finishes his smoke, field strips it and away we go. A while later, we reach our Barracks where we are told to fall out and be prepared to move out in 15 minutes. I wish I could have filmed the mad dash to recover smokes from foot lockers. Remember, 5 weeks have past with open packs of smokes in foot lockers. We are talking stale dried out smokes here. We form up and march around all day with smokes stuck in your sock. Use of pockets was not allowed. No smoke break. How cruel !

The next day, back on the 'Drill Pad' we just knew this would be it. Yep, you did good, 'Light 'Em Up'. 50 cigarettes appear like magic. A quick check, they are all lit. PUT 'EM OUT! What? He is not joking. With tears, 50 cigarettes are field stripped and filters if they had one neatly tucked away. There is talk of murder. That no good (explitive deleted).The next day, 'Rest, light 'em up'. 50 smokes lit and puffing like old engine 97 coming up a grade. Those smokes were lit up like Christmas. Every cigarette was cherry red for half of it's length.

Everyone getting their puffs before we were shut down again. Grey Eyes just stood there watching . A kid to my left fell down he was so dizzy. Then another went down. A few more had to sit before they fell down. Then Grey Eyes started laughing. One guy got sick. Old Grey Eyes said, "Damn Fools"

At the end of training camp, I was one of just a handful waiting for a flight to my Tech School, I asked him, "You do that smoke thing with every group, don't you"? YEP. Ha Ha. I said that was really mean. He said , "Careful Boy, your flight is not here yet."

The Obstacle Course

The words Obstacle Course struck fear in all of us. The first time was a trip. The fear disappeared quickly. I was a lightning fast 6' 140 pounds. I was hardly noticed. It was FUN! The fat guys however had zero Fun.

Wow, I could have done that everyday. The only time it was not fun was one time at the Mine field. It was a field maybe an acre or so that had a lot of barbed wire stretched over it about 18" above ground. Lots of sandbags. That's where the mines were. There were maybe six ways through the mine field, all serpentine. As you ran up to it you just picked one of the routes and without stopping dive on the ground and start crawling as fast as you could.

On this particular day, I hit the dirt and started crawling. About the second curve, I run into a pair of boots. There is no way around. In front of those boots and attached to them is a body that is like a cry baby kid saying I can't make it, over and over. High over this field is a tower with some God Like characters observing what is happening down on Earth. They have not spotted the whiner.

UH OH they see him. Quickly, I put my fingers in my ears, I know what is coming. **KABOOM!** I swear it lifted me off the ground. Dirt and gravel raining down. Holy Moly. Hey, the boots are **GONE**, did they blow him up? No twenty fast feet later, here are the boots again, same whining

KABOOM, gone again. I had learned to plug my ears every time I came to 'Happy Feet'. Five or six times my world was rocked that trip. I had decide to lay back and the next water hazard, that Dude was going for a swim. I never had a chance, they were waiting for him when he came out the other side.

John, who occupied the bunk above me, and I sort of befriended this gangly kid from TN, he had a terrible time with the course. At the end of each trip, he surely did not look like the rest of us. He was filthy because he had fallen in every hazard on the course and was also the last to finish every time.

He was informed that if he didn't finish by a certain time on his final run, he would wash out. John and I said that wouldn't happen. So on that day, we got him between us and if he fell in a hazard, we would very quickly, without ceremony, drag him out . Despite the mess, we made good time. Almost finished, one obstacle left, some big logs across a stream. Easiest obstacle on the course. Most, simply ran across. They were really big logs. The water in this stream was clear because nobody fell in there. Our mountain boy gets half way across, looks around and JUMPS! KASPLASH. What the hell are you doing down there? "The water was clear, I just wanted to get some mud off of me." He passed. Grey Eyes was impressed. He didn't say so, we just knew it.

New Respect for Grey Eyes

It happened on a night march. We were out in the boon docks trekking along this road that went most everywhere. One long line of troupes on each side with the instructors in the middle between their troops.

We were told, we would encounter 'Tear Gas' on the trek and that if you broke ranks and ran, they would drag you back through it. We started down this easy slope that led to a steeper slope down into a small canyon.

In the moonlight, it looked like snow down there. Tear Gas can look like that when there is no wind. COME ON WIND! No such luck. I noticed up ahead, instructors cutting out and taking a walking bridge to the far side well above the Tear Gas. Not Grey Eyes, he went right through it with us yelling not to rub your skin that indeed was on FIRE ! Out the other side with a new found respect for Tear gas and Grey Eyes. My eyes burned, every piece of exposed skin burned. It seemed like 100 times worse than the 'Gas House' we visited a week earlier.

I observed Grey Eyes calmly take out a handkerchief and pat below his eyes just once. Perhaps this is how he got Grey Eyes.

Did you know that Rattlesnakes hate Tear gas? Well, I guess all snakes hate Tear gas. It's just that a Rattlesnake will **TELL** you he hates it. Let me tell you, in the bottom of that canyon there were Rattlesnakes, **LOTS** of them. When they got a whiff of that Tear gas, they were pissed. All of them singing with their tails. It was like a snake symphony. Years later, I can still hear them. Every hair on my body was at attention.

Rumors

Rumors started circulating that one of the Basic trainees was caught having sex with a female recruit in a dumpster. What? How could that be? We were under close scrutiny 24/7. I had seen female recruits in the distance marching some where and I had seen some of them at the Base exchange. They were being watched as close as we were.

I just could not see how this could be. In a dumpster? You gotta be kidding me.

Fast forward about 40 years. I am at San Antonio again, this time for my son Michael's graduation from Basic training. While I was visiting with him, I thought about the 'Dumpster' incident so I asked if he heard about the guy getting caught with the girl in a dumpster? He was amazed that I had heard about it. Was it on the news Dad?

A good story is worth repeating. Ha

I am sure they are still talking about it as you read this.

Chapter 28

USAF Tech School

Escaping the heat and Basic Training, I was on cloud Nine. They shipped me off to school at Chanute AFB just in time for WINTER IN ILLINOIS. Woo Hoo.

I was assigned to a PATS barracks (People Awaiting Technical School) This Barracks was maned by two airmen wearing Green ropes. One level below the almighty Red. These guys were really hard on us. Lots of inspections etc.

Because we were Tech School Airmen, we did not complete basic training in San Antonio. We had to complete Basic training while at Chanute AFB. Three more weeks of Basic, ugh. No, Six more weeks. ½ day at school, ½ day at Basic. Oh well, at least the weeks of waiting for my school was over.

Those were weeks of nice things like Kitchen Patrol also known as K.P. Have you ever seen a mess hall that feeds 6000 at a meal? I worked there.

School was fun, I liked it a lot. For me it was pretty easy. By now winter was setting in and man it was cold. We lived in WWII open bay two story barracks that were Cold.

The only room that was warm was the Barracks commander's room. It was a private room. The barracks commander was one of those green rope guys but not a hard ass like the PATS guys. His function was to make sure we assembled at the proper time and to march us to morning formation with the other Flights.

At Chanute AFB
Learning to become
A Rocket Scientist

Then as a 'Squadron' (Several Flights) we would march to the Mess Hall and then march to school. I decided I was going to become a 'Rope'. My friend Carl had the same thoughts.

Everyday before basic training, our shoes had the best shine and our 'War Suits' had extra starch and the seams would remain sealed shut until just before daily inspection. Gotta brag, WE WERE SHARP. At graduation, both of us were nominated to Rope school.

Things are looking good. Another Three weeks of training learning how to march troupes in a confined area without running them into a wall, all while a Drill instructor is yelling in your ear. All kinds of distractions. Some washed out there. Carl and I both graduated and were each assigned a barracks to govern.

Not only did we each get our own room, we each got a 24/7 gate Pass. We could go to town every night. What a cool perk.

116

Being a 'Rope'

Fun mostly, I got along great with everyone but there was a couple of times when it was tough.

The first was one day a "Runner" was dispatched to my barracks telling me to report to the Squadron commander. When I got there, I saw an Airman (no stripes) standing in the middle of the room. The Commander informed me that this guy had just minutes before been sentenced to one year in the Stockade.

He said this guy had gone AWOL and made it to Cheyenne on the way to California. He turned himself in and because he did that, a recruiter put him on a train on his own, back to Illinois. At the first stop, he got off, cashed his ticket and headed for California again. Caught this time, he was brought back in chains.

The commander asked if I knew where the Stockade was? Yes Sir. Okay, march this guy right down the Center of the street. If he gives you a problem, Take him out. With what? Here's your weapon. It was a beautiful Red and white Baseball bat.

Marching a pace behind and a half step left, that Baseball Bat was cocked and ready to fire. I was certain I was going to have to pull the trigger on that weapon. I was very nervous about this assignment. We didn't make it a hundred yards and this guy starts up with the "Look buddy, yada yada." I halted him right there and in my calmest, most authoritative voice let him know the next words would put him on his knees. Anything more and he would be on his face. It worked. Those were his last words to me .What a relief to get rid of that dude.

Then it was time for the Boxing event. Held every year to find the best boxer from the Base in all weight divisions. Each squadron would field the best squad they could and Box against the other squadrons. The winners from our base would then go to other Air Force Bases and so on.

I was dumb enough to give it a go one year and I thought I was pretty good until,.... In the ring with me is Terry, a kid of Irish decent. We were in the same weight division, 160 to 165 pounds. I had a bit of reach advantage so, I will be okay. They rang the Bell and that was the **last time** I saw Terry . Every time I tried to look, there was leather coming toward my face. Fast and Hard. Being honest, I will tell you, he beat the snot out of me. **Literally and Physically!**

The try out notices are posted everywhere. The first night for practice arrives and I announce to the Barracks that it is clean up time. Floors to buff, showers etc to clean, all the not so fun stuff. This one guy comes to me and says he is off to boxing practice. Is there a 110 Pound division? Oh well, maybe he has more power than it looks like he has. So , every night, he is off to Boxing practice.

One day, I happened to be in the Orderly room picking up some new students to get settled in and I see the First Sarge who is heading up our boxing team. I ask how my boy is doing? He asks who that is. I tell him and he looks confused. He said he had no one with that name. I asked if he got cut from the squad? Nope, never heard of him. Why do you ask? Hmm, ducking all that work Huh? Looks like it.

The Sarge tells me not to say anything, just make sure he was at the gym for the boxing on Saturday. This was the start of the Box-offs, everyone is going to be there for this.

I had asked Carl, my buddy and a couple of other strong arms to be at my Barracks that Saturday morning, just in case there was trouble.

The Barracks begins to empty Saturday morning to see the fights. I stroll through the Barracks and there is my boy lying on his bed. I asked what's Up? You better hurry. He says, "I'm not going, I got cut from the team last night."

I said What? I talked to the Sarge and he said you were doing great. So good in fact, he asked if My friends and I would escort you to the Gym. This was the first time I had ever seen a person pale so quickly. Now get your things and Let's go. This kid was as white as this paper. Arriving at the gym, Sarge was all smiles when he announced a very special non scheduled Bout.

He put this kid in the ring with a really good boxer and he told the kid to fight. If he even thought the kid was taking a Dive, there would be a Court Martial. Time for me to feel bad, this kid got a beating way worse than Terry had given me. The Sarge told me to give him more punishment also. If he balked at that, he would step in.

Word spread quickly and soon, everyone in the barracks knew what this kid had done. They were not happy. I knew I had to come down hard on this guy before his roommates took matters into their own hands.

The guys at the Barracks thought it was pretty awesome that for the next month this kid was cleaning the whole Latrine all by himself.

Lesson learned.

Chapter 29

USAF Abilene

I finished tech school and received orders that I would be stationed at Dyess AFB in Abilene, Texas. Hot, but not as hot as San Antonio. At least my new barracks had cooling. They had water coolers that are effective in a desert environment. My new home was one of the closest barracks to the runway. Just falling asleep, there is a huge roar. It's a B-47 on take off roll. They have a long take off roll. Yikes, how do you sleep thru that?

Minutes later, another one, and another, and on and on. 24/7, B-47's coming and going.

Then the transition happened, brain power I guess. It did not take long and I never heard them again. That was cool.

Several months later, the B-47s left. One morning I was walking to breakfast and there on the Flight Line was a B-52.

Where did that come from? The next morning, there were three of them. Finally there was nearly thirty of them. It seemed like they just sat there. But one day there might be 5 there , the next day ten . Never heard them come or go. One day I looked and there was one actually moving. Looks like he's going to take off. Gotta see this. I'm no aircraft designer, and I do not think the B-52 designer was either. What a gangly looking aircraft. I loved the B-47s with their sleek body and swept wings, a real beauty.

This B-52 taxis out to the runway Pours the fuel to it and it nearly disappeared in black smoke. Slowly, I mean slowly it lumbers down the runway. Good thing there is over three miles of runway. UH OH, he's going to crash for sure. The rear main landing gear lifted off before the forward gear.

What? A plane can't fly like that. The rear main was probably 5 to 6 foot higher than the front. It continued like that even after the gear was up all the way through climb-out. This was the normal flight characteristics of a B-52.

My first day on the job was paperwork. Another FBI check for my 'Top Secret' clearance. The same level that I went through at Tech School. Watching all the news about Hillary passing around classified material on her email server, I remember the stern warnings I received and signed receipts stating that if I leaked one single document, intentionally or unintentionally, it would mean a minimum of 15 years at Leavenworth Prison. (the U.S. Gulag) Two sets of Justice you see. Five days past and I was good to go.......

I was assigned to a crew of various job titles. There was another propulsion tech that I knew from school. The rest were career guys, some had a LOT of stripes.

My first entry into a Missile Silo was intimidating for sure. The Atlas 'F' sits erect in a Silo, when it is about to launch, it is fueled with RP1 (rocket propellant #1) aka kerosene, aka JP4 (jet fuel) and Liquid Oxygen. Then it comes above ground on an elevator for launch.

Past security and into the Silo we go. Not much to see, the missile sitting on the launch elevator that is inside a square enclosure. There is a service elevator down to the engine section. Rather confusing for a while because the engines are all in a vertical position. All the engines at tech school were horizontal. It took a while to get my head around this.

121

During maintenance times, access ramps would be lowered to work on the missile at different points. We rode the elevator up to the warhead level. Opening the door, there it was, a 6 Megaton Nuke. Holy moly, **More explosive power than all the bombs that were dropped in all the wars** right in front of me. No mock-up, not a Dummy. The real deal right there. Breathless would be a good word. **I laid my hands on it.** A sight that lives with me today.

JFK

I was called in one day and was told that the President of the United States was coming to Dyess AFB and part of his tour was to be our unit. I was to be there in Class A uniform to answer any questions he might have about the engine systems. (There was a missile in the hangar for him to see.)

I was briefed on his itinerary. He would be in Dallas doing the political stuff then go to Carswell AFB in Ft Worth, then fly to Abilene to see me.

Sad to say, He didn't make it.

Another Visitor

I had a similar task when Jimmy Stewart came to town. He was to tour our facility.

122

What? They let movie stars do that? In this case , yes. You see Jimmie Stewart was also a Major General in the Air Force reserves. **He did make it to see me**. He walked up to the engine pod, looked in and said, How are you Airman? Very well Sir. Looking at the engines again, he said, "That's very impressive". Yes Sir. He said, "Thank You Airman" and off he went.

Jimmy Stewart was a really good Man. I was impressed with his kindness and "Down to Earth" conversation. Nothing fake about that man.

The Missile

The missile itself was a strange critter. It was a very thin Stainless Steel Balloon. The skin was about the thickness of a Dime and there was no internal structure.

The top 2/3rds was Liquid oxygen tank the bottom 1/3rd RP1 storage. The ONLY thing keeping it looking like a missile was internal Pressure, 4-6 PSI. dump all the pressure and it folds like a cheap suit.

Attached to the bottom of this was my department, The engines. Two huge Booster engines and one big Sustainer engine. On the sides of the missile were two Vernier engines that were very small. They were used for direction control. The engine pod was a maze of tubing and wiring.

Personal Observations

Having described the above, I started seeing flaws here.

a) if this missile is fueled below ground, then raised on an elevator that was not fast, a lot of time has elapsed.

b) Chemistry. Mixing a hydrocarbon with liquid oxygen is a potential disaster.

c) The propulsion system was so complex, there was thousands of scenarios that could lead to a disaster.

d) Once fueled, the missile was above ground and the countdown begins. Any decent sniper could bring this missile down from a mile away. Sort of a giant sitting Duck.

Being worked to Death

A big push began to get our Squadron operational as soon as possible. We were putting missiles into the Green, ie: ready for war as fast as possible. Not good enough, an order came down that there would be no more Leaves granted and everyone would work 18 hours on with 10 hours off everyday until we were fully operational. I said hey, some genius thinks there is 28 hours in a day. Boy, was I wrong.

Shifts went something like this. Go to the hanger, meet my crew, get our work assignment and drive to the missile site. Probably night time, down we go. Come out 16 hours later, it's dark. Back to the base, eat, go to sleep. Wake up, it's dark, do it all again.

If you will look at a clock and put your fingers to work, you will soon see, Crap, those guys were working a different shift shift EVERY day.

Three months of this. All of us first term guys were always saying to each other, " I'm having so much fun, where's the paper work, I want to reenlist." One day, I heard that statement on the P.A. System at a launch site. It was followed by a stern voice demanding to know who said that! Sure, like someone was going to say, It was me, I did it.

Unaware of what was going on in other shops of our squadron. Some guy went to his senior Sarge and asked for time off because he was going crazy. The Sarge said, he couldn't give him time off, nobody was getting that. The kid said get me an appointment with the Commander, I have to have some time off. He was informed harshly that was not going to happen. What can I do? The kid asks. Write your congressman, now get out of here. This kid wrote his congressman describing in detail what was happening. Like I said, we were unaware.

Then one day, we arrive at this missile site and down we go. On the job for an hour or so, we are summoned to the Launch Control center. We are told to report back to the Base ASAP. What? We just got here. Just Go!

Back at the Base, we are met by this Lt. Col., he says we have three days off, report back for work in three days at 8am. What? Just Go he said.

Wow, back at the Barracks, I saw friends I had not seen in months. What's going on? Nobody knew. Three days later, the hanger bay is full of troops. The Commander will speak in a moment. Here comes a Bird Col. Everyone Pops to. Hey, that's not our commander. **He is now!** He climbs up on the engine platform and announces that from that day forward, his door is always open to us to talk to him about anything, work, girlfriends, anything. UNDERSTOOD? Then he announces we all had another three days off. Woo Hoo.

You probably guessed it. The former Bird Col. Figured it out that if his Squadron was the First Atlas 'F' Squadron to become fully operational, he was to become a General very quickly. **It got him early retirement instead.** All because this kid took the advice of his boss and wrote his congressman. A phone call to the Pentagon by that Congressman, confirmed they did not know what was happening down there in Texas.

Thanks kid, I appreciated the time off.

Time to Relocate

Not much more than a year after we got all the Atlas missiles ready for war, There was a buzz starting that the mighty Atlas was going Bye Bye. I kind of had that figured. We were riding a dead horse. In a year and a half, only one Airman 2nd class had been promoted to Airman 1$^{st.}$

Sure enough, word comes that nine guys from the engine shop are going to be retrained into the Minuteman ICBM field. My roommate and I were the two senior airmen and so It was certain we would go. We were told that 7 would go to Whiteman AFB in Missouri. 2 would go to Minot North Dakota. Any Volunteers? My roommate says, we are going anyhow, lets volunteer. Surely they wouldn't send a volunteer to North Dakota. He volunteers with one other guy. You can guess what happened then.

I'm packing for Missouri.

My Roommate is buying Wool Socks

Chapter 30

USAF Knob Noster

Knob Noster, Missouri, home of Whiteman Air Force Base. Who names a town Knob Noster? I guess all the other names were taken.

Well, I'm going back to Chanute AFB in Illinois for another three months of training. The good news is that it's summer time. Not so fast boy, it's going to be 3 months before the school is open for me. What will I be doing until then? Just about anything. Then I got lucky, sort of.

The Wild Blue Yonder

A runner came to my barracks with a note saying I was to report to Base Operations the following morning and be prepared to be gone TDY for three days. What? Where?

The next morning I was told I was being assigned to a C-123 temporarily due to a sick crew guy. Yea! What's a C-123? I found out, it is a very old twin engine (Reciprocating engines) cargo hauler that was supposed to be the miracle replacement for the WWII C-119 aka flying box car. It was not a good idea. It looks a lot like a C-130 except, it is like 3/4 scale.

C123

I meet the crew, they were not a happy crew. What, these are the 'Fly Boys', Fun etc. Then I meet the Pilot. What a grouch. I think he had to consult the rule book before returning a salute. So we load up. Mostly troops headed for Vandenberg AFB Calif.

Woo Hoo, I'm airborne! This thing is LOUD ! Sure seemed like we used a whole bunch of runway to get into the air. It was so loud, hand

127

signals or notes were the only form of communication.

The crew hated this plane and their skipper. So much so, I saw they were observing the pilot for some reason. Okay, I get it with a smile. A C-123 is a mechanical airplane. Everything is done by hand. The 'Flight Deck' was 3-4 feet higher than the cargo deck. The crew could watch the pilot trimming the flight controls, elevator and rudder to get the plane to fly straight and level. This took some time.

Finally completed, the pilot could take his hands and feet off the controls. At this point, the crew gestured to me to follow them. They all got up and walked to the rear of the plane and sat on one side.

Forward on the flight deck, the pilot could be seen again starting the trim process. Some time later, the trimming once again complete, the whole crew was on the move again. Over and over. There is no telling how many work orders were written for faulty trim controls.

Almost forgot, we had an Airman with a trashcan between his legs before we got off the runway... Gag me !

We arrive in California and shut off those engines. What, I can still hear them. They were running in my mind for several hours.

I see they have that kid dragging his trashcan to be cleaned by himself.

A day later, we head home to Knob Noster. Not so fast, take off roll is aborted. What? Try again. Nope. Third try, we are in the air. Boy, do I feel safe. At Pre-flight we are told of severe turbulence over the Mojave desert. Because of this, we plan on flying South for a while then head East. Leaving at 7am, well, 7:30 actually, weather should be okay. We flew South for a long time. We turn East and a while later, Yellow light comes on.

Oh boy, put the Parachutes on. Let me tell you, after a few hours of that, you are sick of them. The only good part was that if that jump light went on, and it is a choice between flying into a mountain or jumping, I'm out of there. Here comes the heat turbulence. Boom, bang, over and over. It finally smoothed out.

It's getting dark, where are we? Looking out, I knew that was not Missouri down there. Turns out that after a whole day of flying, we were safely on the ground at Davis Montham AFB in Tucson Az. What fun.

We made the rest of the trip okay. I got back to my room and my roommate asked how my flight was? I shouted at him (because I could still hear engines), "If I have to do that again, I'm going AWOL".

The C-130

Not long after the above trip, another runner came looking for me. Pack your gear, be prepared to be gone for 10 days. The runner said he was to wait while I packed and then deliver me to Base Ops.

No opportunity to go AWOL. Base Operations told this kid to deliver me to the flight line. What a relief when we pulled up to a C-130

I meet the crew and these guys were happy. What I expected with a flight crew. One of the load master guys said I would be working with him because his partner tore up a finger somehow. What will I be doing? He said he would show me how to adjust a 'Tie-down' strap. The same thing I would have learned in 4 weeks of loadmaster school. Ha Ha. He also said there was going to be trouble when the Captain arrived. What? He said to just watch.

A staff car pulls up and the Captain steps out, walks up to the plane and this super sarge (one of those that had stripes from his shoulder to elbow) ground chief who hands him a clipboard with the manifest on it. The plane was fully loaded plus we were taking U.S. Army trainees to Panama for jungle training.

The Captain says, "This plane is overloaded sarge". No sir he says, there is a lot of cargo, but the weight is okay.

Who's flying this plane sarge? You are sir. That's right sarge. What are those crates on the loading ramp? Sarge says, it's these items sir, pointing at the manifest. The Captain reaches to the sarge and takes a pencil from his pocket, draws lines through those items and says , "Now get that stuff off my plane". I thought the veins in the sarge's neck were about to rupture.

There will be hell to pay over this. The captain says Did you mean to say there will be hell to pay over this, **SIR?**" Sorry sir, yes sir. Okay sarge, now get moving. The ground boys unloaded and hauled off the cargo for the next flight. The crew was all chuckles. The captain gets in his car and drives off. Where's he going? He'll be right back. More chuckles.

A few minutes later, I hear this little motorcycle and here is the captain driving it right onto the airplane with a Golf cart and golf clubs on the back like a small trailer. He says, Strap her down boys, we gotta get out of here **fast**. One hell of a fast pre-flight check.

The Captain briefed his passengers after we took off. A stretch of the rules I would say. I remember a couple of things about the briefing. First was he pointed out the panic lights. The first being to chute Up, the second was to jump. He pointed to the row of parachutes and says, the first one is mine , the second is the co-pilot etc all the way to me. He said , you will see that leaves one chute for you guys. May the best man win. There were at least 40 Army guys on board. He said, " Don't worry about the 'Jump' light", Just watch out the small windows, You will see something go by, That will be me, try to keep up".

He also said not to worry about jumping because we would be over water all the way to Panama, so in the case of emergency, we would land at sea. Now, I know what you are thinking, this plane really looks like a boat. When landing in the water, there will be two impacts, the first when we contact water, the second is when this plane breaks in half. Try to stay away from the break point.

I'm thinking he must have been in training to become a Pilot for Southwest Airlines.

A while later, I'm told the pilot wants to talk to me. What? I go to the flight deck and I am instructed to sit in the Flight engineer seat. It is located in the middle above and behind the pilots. The view is amazing. The pilot turns and introduces himself and the rest of the flight guys. At one point, he asked if I liked flying and I said sure, I had just been licensed to fly a Cessna 172. He said awesome.

He got up and told me to sit in his seat. He told the Copilot to let me have it. I was scared to death. Straight and Level baby. Then he said, "I thought you said you could fly?" Come on, let's fly. Oh Wow, around the clouds we go. Awesome! Flying around and between huge clouds is nothing short of spectacular from the front seat of a C130. The Navigator was busy now. I will never, ever forget that experience.

Howard AFB Panama

Everyone has seen the Tarzan movies with the birds and monkeys screaming in the background? I can verify it is true.

When we shut down those engines at Howard Air Force Base Panama, Two things invaded my senses. The intense humidity and the noise of the jungle. You can hear 'Howler' monkeys and screaming birds from a mile away. They are that loud. Amazing. Things grow fast there. It rains every day. Average temp in the summer is 86 degrees. Average temp in the winter is 82 degrees. They are constantly cutting the jungle back. They say if nothing was cut, you would never find the base in a year's time. I believe that.

On We Went

I was fortunate to spend three months with these guys. We went many places. The pilot let me fly a lot and always said I was going to learn to land next. It didn't happen. I even got to make a visit to DaNang VietNam. Man what a Tourist Resort. Yep, just like the movies. Everyone stationed in VietNam had mental issues of some sort. I was very uncomfortable around them.

Because of wind conditions, we had to make an approach from inland. I had no idea that a plane that big could make an approach that steep. All because there were these bad guys with black pajamas running around out there on the approach path. They said we were shot at, but a close inspection of the aircraft revealed nothing.

Oh yeah, our cargo on that trip was ammo crates and "Military Advisers". They were some scary dudes. Nobody talked to them. They didn't even talk to each other. Scary! I think CIA Professional Killers would be closer to the truth.

VietNam was the only place the Pilot's scooter and golf cart did not go. It had to be left behind in Guam. I think he was having withdrawal symptoms by the time we got back.

Alas, after three months, my orders came through for tech school in Illinois. Oh Joy, just in time for winter in Illinois. I have knowledge now of why those folks become 'Winter Texans'.

Just three months and yet, it was an emotional departure from my flight crew. Thanks guys for the BEST three months of my military career. I learned the art of drinking Martinis with them. I have since lost that talent.

Later in life, I had to retrieve my DD214 Form (discharge papers) to prove I had received an Honorable Discharge. I was asked if I was a VietNam vet. There is no mention of my one day visit to the tourist resort of DaNang. I found that it could be noted if they can find records of my TDY assignments. Don't hold your breath they said. I kind of felt guilty about being there only one day anyhow.

A quick Funny

My friend Tom and I earned our private pilot license while we were at Whiteman. We would fly some distance to get a hamburger from a place someone said was really good.

On one of our trips, we were headed back to Whiteman and we heard an obvious rookie air traffic controller. He was speaking very slowly a distinctly. Tom was at the controls and he broke into a grin.

When it was our turn, Tom keyed the mike and said, (I wish I could do   this   really   fast   ) ahwhitemantowercessna7792tango15mileseastenteringtrafficpatternover There is no way I could ever talk that fast. He sounded like a TV voice doing the gibberish disclaimer at the end a commercial. A considerable pause and the same voice gives us barometer, wind speed and all the right and proper stuff. It took a long time.

All was fine until we were turning Final. This kid gives final wind etc. Then he says, 7792 Tango report gear down and locked. Tom never skipped a beat, 'Roger tower, gear down and welded'. A Cessna 172 has fixed gear you see. A pause and a very serious authoritative voice comes on and says, "Nine Two Tango, call the tower by phone when you reach your hanger". Click. UH OH.

We taxi up and step out. About two steps were taken and we hear the phone ringing. Tom said he thought it might be for **me**. I said, 'You're on your own'. Tom put his hand on the phone, stared at it for a moment then picked it up and said Hello. After that it was a constant stream of yes sir, no sir, yes sir, yes sir on and on. Tom hung up and said the Major in the tower has no sense of humor. Let's go have a beer.

That was Tom, the funniest guy ever. When I first saw Toni, who I would later Marry, I had told Tom, she's too pretty to be interested in me. He said, "This is your one shot, you better Go For It." He was the 'Best Man' at my wedding. Tom continued on with his flying all the way through to multi engine jets. He was employed by the FAA doing Boeing 737 pilot certifications until he retired.

Chapter 31

USAF Minuteman

Having survived another brutal winter in Illinois, it's back to Knob Noster. Tech school was pretty easy because the Minuteman missile is quite similar to a 4th of July skyrocket. Not a whole lot that can go wrong. I was reunited with a lot of old friends from the Atlas program at school. That was a good thing.

Funnies

I was assigned to a good crew. All career guys except for Russell and myself. One of the crew, a SSGT, was a funny guy. He kept us laughing even during the worst of times. He had funny made-up names for most everything. These names became the generic names that we used everyday. This is the basis for the following story.

We had heard rumors that some powerful people were coming to see the Minuteman missile set up. Congressmen, a Senator and Generals. Just great, our crew was selected for the 'Dog & Pony' show. The 'Show' was to be as follows. Our crew was to open a silo, pull the warhead and guidance package. Then an installer group would pull the missile. Next they would reinstall the missile and we would reinstall the guidance package. (It fits between the missile and the warhead) Then reinstall the warhead. We would do the basic target alignment which would complete our portion.

Problems started early. Something broke so the ssgt headed back to base to get a replacement. I don't remember the original problem. Work continued while the sarge was gone until another problem occurred.

To open the huge concrete door covering the Silo, A large piston has to be pulled that locks the door closed. During wartime, this is done with a powder charge. During maintenance, nitrogen is used. On this occasion, our regulator failed. My Crew Chief told me to go upstairs (above ground) and call the sarge to bring a replacement.

Remember the funny names? I come out of the silo to use the truck radio and here comes the Sargent Major (The ranking NCO that sucks up to the Generals) he asks, what's going on Airman? Without thinking or reaction, I said "We have a bad FRUNISENSE regulator" and continued my walk.

Speechless, he followed me. I am certain he was suspicious. I better make this good. I got on the radio to the sarge and told him we had a broken regulator. Over the radio, the sarge says, "The Frunisense regulator?" I said 10-4 on the Frunisense regulator. Reply, 10-4, I'll swing by the shop and bring a replacement. Walking back to go down into the silo, I saw a General approaching with three other 'Suits'. General to the Sargent Major, "What's going on sarge?" He says, " They have a defective frunisense regulator sir." Very good Sarge. Put that in the report........ Nearly wet myself. I wonder if he spelled that correctly.

Truck Drivers Needed

The routine of setting up a missile site for our crew consisted of a convoy of three vehicles. A semi truck that carried the Guidance package and Warhead.

This vehicle would be parked over the silo and a hoist inside would lower the guidance package from its belly onto the missile and then the same for the warhead.

The second vehicle was a 6 passenger support van carrying all the gear required for our work. The third vehicle was a six passenger pick up.

When carrying a Nuke, 45mph was the rule and we would have to stop and check the load at prescribed intervals. Kind of fun for Russ and I because we could jump out with our .30 cal carbines ready for some action. (We were all armed and the arms were loaded). In some cases, it was a LONG ride to a missile site. A good time for a nap.

Our Semi driver was a Gung-Ho second term A1C. He never gave me much confidence with his ability. It would take forever for him to position the trailer 'Just so' over a Silo. Our crew chief got tired of that and one day told Russ and I to go to the motor pool and get our semi drivers license. Russ and I talked it over and decided that would be the end of our sleep time. So off to testing. I turned that steering wheel so many times , my arms were hurting. We crushed every orange 'Snow cone' we could.

I wish I could have taken a photo of the tracks in that parking lot. We damaged a lot of that parking lot also. The Motor pool guy said to get out of there. Failed ! The worst drivers he had ever seen. Our crew chief was not pleased.

It had to happen. Not long later, we are on the way to a new site. We have a map that is hand made at base operations. We came to this intersection out in the farmland. The map says to go straight ahead on this gravel road. Hmm, different, usually a gravel road going to missile sites have been greatly improved by the Government. Rather like a gravel super highway.

Not this one. Pretty narrow. Has to be correct. Press on. Hmm, getting more narrow. About a mile into it, and it is more like a farm lane. STOP! Has to be wrong. Ditches on both sides, no place to turn around. Gotta back it out. About a Mile? Yep. Gung Ho backs up about 5 feet and is going in the ditch. A serious No No with a Nuke on board. Pull forward 4 feet, back 5, forward 4, over and over.

A tap on my shoulder. I turn to look eye to eye with the chief. He says for me to get in that G.D. truck and back that S.O.B. out of here! I could see this was not a good time to argue.

The Chief talked to me a lot about 'farm life'. So he knew I could drive. I couldn't help it, I grinned when I said, get out of the truck dude. Sarge says so. Lots of bitching. Talk to the chief dude. I backed the semi out and the chief never asked me to get my license again.

Up Against the Wall Red Neck Mother !

When I started training for the Minuteman, I found that I would need yet another security clearance. This time it was for a Top Secret Crypto clearance. The Big Daddy of Clearances. The same as Hillary has.

The main difference is that we were informed if we leaked one piece of classified information, accidentally or intentionally, it was Leavenworth baby. Okay, this means a ton of paperwork to fill out for the FBI & OSI. How many times do I have to do this? This is the fourth time. The First was to get a Confidential clearance. The second time was to get a Secret clearance. The third was for Top Secret. Now it is to get a Top Secret Crypto Clearance.

Going home on leave, I had several people ask what I was doing because these guys in suits were asking a lot of questions about me. Not the best feeling I have ever had.

I guess the answers were good because I was cleared. I was issued two codes, one a clear text that I could speak out loud. A series of numbers. The other code was secret text, another series of numbers.

These had to be memorized and never to be shared outside of my duties. Why you ask? Pretty simple actually. A Minuteman Missile site is unmanned and therefore has a very elaborate security system.

Here is how it became **Up Against The Wall.** Job assignment to go to a specific Missile site. Off to Base Operations. I am issued a code book with the daily numbers. Just a small book that has numerous numbers. One set of numbers per page. Get in the truck and head out.

Before reaching the gate at the site, we call in by radio and ask permission to break outer security. (The Gate) Permission granted, we unlock the gate and an alarm sounds back at a Launch compound.

We now have 3 minutes to enter the site, go to the underground support building, (triangulation radar alarm sounds) at the Launch center, unlock the hatch (another alarm), go down the ladder and pick up the phone on the wall. My boss goes first. He gives his Clear Text code over the phone. Launch center now knows who he is supposed to be, they instruct him to go to a certain page in his book and subtract.

This means, he turns to say page 22 and there is a number on that page. He puts his secret number on that page and subtracts his number from the one on the page. He does that and gives the answer over the phone.

Launch Control guys do the same to make sure we are not Commies. Next, it's my turn, **But Wait, they ask him to go to another page and repeat**. Uh Oh, a slight delay and he hands me the phone.

I hear other voices in the Launch center. Rather unusual. I go through the same drill. Repeat again. **UH OH, Sarge back on the line, YES SIR, YES SIR, YES SIR.** He hangs up and says OUTSIDE, NOW! Okay, should we lock the gate? He says he thinks others will handle that.

A LONG five minutes passes and then I hear them, **SIRENS! We see them coming. Sarge says EVERYBODY OUT OF THE TRUCKS. It's UP AGAINST THE FENCE RED NECK MOTHERS.**

These guys were serious. They fanned out sort of surrounding us. All heavily armed and the Arms were loaded and aimed at me. YIKES.

Not so gently removed from the fence and onto the ground. Checked for weapons etc.

After about an hour of sitting on rocks someone figured it out that either we or the Launch Center were issued the wrong code books. Bottom line, the system works.

O.R.I.

O.R.I. Operational Readiness Inspection. When a base declares a Missile is ready for war, SAC Hq. puts that site on ready alert. From time to time, The system is tested.

All missiles that are "Ready" are placed on chips and go in a hat. Someone reaches in and draws a chip. If that chip says for example, Whiteman AFB flight F site 9, We go to that site under the prying eyes of the inspectors and pull the warhead. It goes back to the Nuke Bunker. Then the guidance package is pulled along with the missile and they are loaded on an aircraft and flown to Vandenberg AFB in California.

Our crew from Whiteman installs the missile, guidance package and dummy warhead. No maintenance is allowed. The target and alignment does the final tweaking and then the launch occurs on the Pacific range. It's 9000 miles to the target near Hawaii.

My crew was selected for two of theses launches. The first was interesting for sure, but we got to view it from more than five miles away. Less than what we hoped to see.

Vandenberg missile launch sites are right at the base of the mountains along the Pacific. There is just a strip of land between the mountains and the Ocean. While we were installing the missile for our second launch, we noticed a camera bunker on the hillside overlooking our site. It was too close to be used during a launch from that site.

Hmmm, if we had someone drop us off up there before daylight, we could hide until launch. What a great idea. Come launch day, here we are, three of us hiding in this 'A' frame bunker. Two hours before launch, here comes two helicopters. They slowly circle the launch site looking for people then start circling in bigger and bigger circles. One came by us close enough to hit with a slingshot. Not seeing anything , the choppers head out to sea and hover around the Russian fishing trawler that has appeared from somewhere.

We could hear the countdown from the speakers at our site. Starting to think we might be a bit close. One minute! We sneak out to the edge. Waiting to see the silo door slide open at 30 seconds. How fast can a door that weighs 80 tons open? WOW, big sand cloud when the door hits the sand bags that were there to stop it. Oh My, looking down into the Silo, we see the warhead. Frightened now. What have we done? BAROOM! Smoke and Fire shooting up past us. Then, there she is passing by making so much noise, covering your ears did nothing. Dirt and sand raining down on us. I have done a lot of crazy things, but I have never been as scared as I was that day. If for some reason that missile would have failed in the first 5 seconds, they would never have found us.

Seconds later, we ran out to see the missile pitch over and head for Hawaii. That was an amazing sight to see, because as the missile pitched to the Southwest. an Air Force F-104 camera plane came streaking in to fly a parallel course for quite a while as the missile was cranking up to it's 22,000 mph speed.

Our best shot from 9,000 miles away was 15 feet left and 150 feet short of the target. Considering the real warhead would leave a hole the size of Rhode Island, that is very accurate.

The sight of that missile passing in front of that bunker is permanent in my mind. Kind of like a topless girl on a sailboat. Not the most brilliant thing I have ever done.

Chapter 32

USAF Toni

Being stationed at Knob Noster did not afford a great social experience. If you had a craving for a girl with teeth, you did not go local. So, that left us with Warrensburg, home of Southwest Missouri State and pretty girls.

One night, my fiends were going to the Pizza Villa, the favorite watering hole in Warrensburg. Actually, it was the only watering hole. If pretty girls were out, that's where they were apt to be.

The beer was cold, the band was good and there she was. Her name was Toni and she was with three friends. I asked her to dance and she said yes. It was Toni and I from that night on. The rest as they say is History. It was fast and it was good.

She moved to New York and shared an apartment with my friend Jim's girlfriend Patti. We were married in Riverside California. We lived in Ransomville until I was transferred to Houston Texas at the beginning of 1972.

Sadly, our marriage did not last. She did give me two sons that are the closest to my heart. For many years, I blamed her for our marriage falling apart. I finally realized that I did not know how to be a good husband and Father. I am indeed sorry for the role I played in the destruction of our marriage.

Today, I try to be a good father, a good husband, a good grandfather and a good Man. Today, Toni and I remain friends and probably get along better than when we were married. We have a number of grandchildren that we Love. (Most of the time)

When the boys reached junior high school, they came to live with me. I will forever be thankful to her for that.

Chapter 33
Jeffrey

Jeffrey, my first born son. Mom was in labor with him for 24 hours. As a first time father, I was totally unprepared for that. I can't even imagine what his mother endured. When we first got to the labor room, a woman in the next room let out the most horrific scream ever heard. Uh Oh. Are we next? It got to be nearly comical. This woman next door called her husband all kinds of bad names that I will not repeat here. "Look what you have done to me" would be a mild example. I was prepared to be thrown under the train at any moment. It didn't happen.

The next day, I found out my friend Jim and his wife were at the same hospital at the same time. We both had sons born on the same day at the same Hospital. Cool.

When we took Jeff home from the hospital, we were a bit worried about how our Golden Retriever 'Kerry' would tolerate a baby.

Kerry had been our only family for some time. We put Jeff in his crib and backed up ready to intervene if needed. Kerry stood on his hind legs for some time looking into the crib. You could just see it, Kerry accepted that he now had a brother. He laid down by the crib and stayed there.

Kerry would stay there until it was time to eat or go outside. When he would come back inside, he would run through the house, stand up to make sure Jeff was still safe and then he would lay down for another tour of being a guard dog.

There were no baby monitors in those days and we did not need one. In the middle of the night, if Jeff was hungry or needed changing, Kerry would run to our room and have a fit until Jeff was quiet again.

When Jeff started crawling, he discovered that Kerry was a retriever. He would roll a golf ball and Kerry would chase it and bring it back. Over and over this game would continue. After about 50 retrieves, Kerry would be exhausted so he would dutifully return the golf ball to Jeff but he would roll the ball way back in his mouth. Jeff figured that out quickly.

He would grab the dogs tongue with one hand and pull. With his other hand , he would reach in the dogs throat and the game was back in play. I was the villain that would end the game by making the ball disappear.

Not long after he was crawling, Jeff approached Kerry while he was eating. Kerry growled and I severely disciplined my dog.

After that day, if Kerry saw Jeff approach his dinner bowl, he would back off and let Jeff have all the Gravy Train he wanted.

Soon Jeff was wanting to become erect, so it was for Kerry to teach him. Kerry, always at Jeff's side, would stand still while Jeff got a couple hands full of dog hair and would pull himself erect. You could see it in Kerry's face that it really hurt. Once erect, Jeff would take a step and so would Kerry.

Not long, and it was was all over the house, Jeff and his Dog. So it was that my Hunting dog discarded me for Jeff.

Early on, it became apparent that Jeff was an independent soul. We had to keep an eye on him or he would just wander off having fun all by himself.

Once in a large department store, he started off by himself, I decided to let him go and follow out of sight. One hour later, not one bit frightened, he is still walking and looking. As a kid, I would have been horrified. Not Jeff.

My biggest scare came one afternoon when we had a rare treat and went to the movies. We had a babysitter that lived next door. When we came home, she was sitting on our front porch. We asked the usual, any problems etc. Then, where is he? Uh Oh, no where to be seen.

The sitter goes ballistic and so do Jeff's parents ! Our neighbors have a pool that is not fenced off. I raced over to it and I did not want to look in it. Thank God, he was not in there. More frantic searching.

I found him! Sound asleep in his sand box laying against the front wall where he could not be seen from the yard. It took a long time to get our hearts and our sitter under control. I **Came of Age that day.**

Life was never boring with Jeff. All through his growing years, It was an exciting time. Fishing, hunting, trapping and baseball. Lots of fond memories for this father.

145

It is note worthy to mention Jeff's skill at skinning a trapped animal. So slow and meticulous, it would drive me up a wall. The good part was, when he was finished, the pelt would be Perfect! You could not find a flaw anywhere. Zero fat, zero flesh, zero nicks or holes, Just Perfect.

The Hunters

188

Undefeated Baytown City Champions

It is with great pride, that I got to see Jeff and Michael play baseball on the first team ever from Baytown to have a perfect baseball season with 12 wins, no losses an no ties. Well done Boys.

So many great times fishing and hunting. I can never remember a time when we caught nothing.

MMMM Fish sticks
For Supper

There were times we caught so many fish, you just would not believe me. I will mention a time we caught so many fish, that Dad was throwing fish off the back of our boat as fast as the boys were throwing them at me from the front.

Love you always

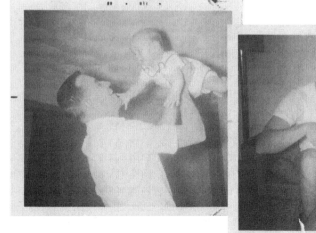

Chapter 34
Michael

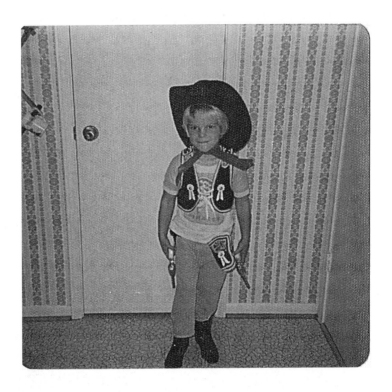

Michael, my second son that became more than a son. When he was born, I thought I was more prepared to be a father. I was wrong. When Jeff was born, it was 24 hours in the labor room. I was told the second child would come much faster. Wrong! 36 hours of labor. Good Lord, how did she do it?

It quickly developed that the first born, Jeffrey, was easy. Michael was anything but easy. For example, when Jeff would be finished with a meal, a simple wipe with a paper napkin and he was clean. Michael would at times simply be carried to the shower where Dad and Michael would shower together. It was that messy.

I suffered with him through a bout with pneumonia before he could talk. That was a very painful time for me. I **came of age** with that episode. I learned a lot about myself and what it was like being a father at that time.

During the time Michael was in the Hospital with pneumonia, something happened that told us he was going to be okay. We had gone down to the cafeteria to eat. Getting back on the elevator to go back up, a maintenance man got on the elevator with his tool box. A nurse asks him what was up? He said, "Some little kid has stuffed a toy in a ventilator machine". Mom and dad look at each other with a knowing look. Sure enough, he gets off on our floor. We hang back and there he goes, right into Michael's room. UH OH, how much does a ventilator cost?

Growing up, Michael was a complete opposite of Jeff. Out in public, he was clingy. Never let go. It was a good thing. Today, he still holds close to everyone he loves. It is a **very** good thing.

As with Jeff, Michael grew up with a close attachment to hunting fishing and trapping. You will read much more about him in other chapters of this book.

It was pretty cool that I got to play a lot of softball with boys. Lots of fun playing on the same team with your sons.

The End of Michael's Toyota Celica

CAR OVERTURNS OFF TEXAS

TWO BAYTOWN police officers, left, and a Baytown wrecker driver, right, prepare to move a 1979 Toyota Celica from the ditch along the 100 block of West Texas between Price Street and Goose Creek. Standing in the center is Bob Schultz of 2102 Cedar Brake, the father of the car's driver, 17-year-old Michael Edward year-old Gern Lynn Mickel of 407 E. Pearce, were uninjured after the car, which was eastbound on West Texas, went out of control, hit a curb and turned over in the ditch. The accident happened at about 9 a.m. Friday. See related photo on page 12-A.

This wreck got Dad's photo on the front page of the Newspaper. No serious injuries so it was just the loss of his car.

150

Funnies

I wake up, my phone is ringing. What time is it? Clock says 2am. What? Baytown PD. What?

Over the Phone: "Do you know where your son is?" Me: "I assume he is not in bed asleep where he is supposed to be". BPD: "That's a fact sir".

Me: "Where is he?" BPD, gives me location. BPD: "We don't want to get him in trouble sir, it's just that it is suspicious seeing a boy on a bicycle at 2am".

Let me say at this point, Michael was 16 years old. He does not have a bicycle and would not dare be seen on a bicycle. Wait, he does have a bicycle, but it's his old 20" kids' bike that is outside with flat tires and half the handle bar is broken off.

Me: "Where did you say he was?" Okay, I got it now. **Our house →** **where he is → girl friend.** All in a straight line............ :-) Got it.

BPD: "Do you want us to bring him home?" Me: "Just send him home, I will be waiting." BPD: "Yes sir." Waiting in the driveway, here he comes peddling fast on a one handle bar bicycle carrying a TIRE PUMP in the other hand. Really cool, 10 feet behind him is a patrol car lit up like a Christmas tree.

During this event, waiting for his arrival, I am thinking there is no way I can punish him for something I have done myself.

He bails out off the bike, walks up and says, (**This was perfect**). "Dad, I know you are not going to believe this, but I just couldn't sleep so I went for a bicycle ride to get some exercise." (**I said Perfect, because I now had grounds to punish him for telling Lies to me.**) Me, "That's right son, I don't believe you." "Go in the house, I will deal with you in a minute."

Michael, "Yes sir." A correct answer.

Police officer walks up and takes Michael's side. He says, "I hate getting Michael in trouble because he seems like a nice kid." I said "Not to worry."

Through all this, someone was standing with me that was the one who I used to sneak out to visit. What goes around, comes around. Ha

Bending Bending

When Michael was younger, he was always asking about things done in my youth. On this day, we were hunting in the Sam Houston National Forest. We came upon a small ravine that had a tiny stream in the bottom. I told Michael that as a boy, we used to climb a **Willow** tree to cross a stream such as this. What? Sure son, we would climb the tree and it would start to bend. The higher we went, the more the bend. Finally, the tree would bend enough to deposit us on the other side of the stream. A lot of Fun. Michael has to do this. A perfect tree is found about 4" in diameter. Michael starts climbing the **PINE** tree. He gets a substantial distance up the tree and it begins to bend. A bit higher, more bend.

152

He's got it going in the right direction. A bit higher, he shifts around so he is on the high side of the **PINE** tree. Higher still, it is clear the tree is lining up perfectly. He's got it to 45 degrees. Climbing is much easier now, UNTIL.....

Either that was a rifle shot or the **PINE** tree has broken. Yep, it's the tree and down she comes fast. Michael astride like a champion Buckeroo. I did notice his eyes were rather large as he passed by.

The tree crosses the stream perfectly, Michael riding waving his cowboy hat like a championship Rodeo rider. Well, the part about the cowboy hat was not true.

The tree lands with a thud. Michael still on board but he was only half way across the stream. The worst part was he was still a few feet above the water. He was speaking in Soprano tones as he rolled off the side and fell in the water.

So the lesson was learned, **Willow** is a much more flexible wood than **PINE** !

Noteworthy , there was no Permanent damage done. He gave me two grandsons.

Love You Son.

Chapter 35

Shipwreck

SS Leaky Teakie

When the boys got a little bigger and before girls, hunting and fishing was their whole world. This is the story about their dad letting the boys talk him into a fishing trip when a voice in the back of my head was screaming,"DON"T DO IT"!

We had a fabulous Bass boat at the time. It was a Sears 14 foot aluminum semi-V rated for a Seven hp motor.

The problem with seven hp and three fisherman is, it becomes a barge. The solution, Twenty five horse power by Mercury, that equals

FAST ! It was so fast, you had to be very careful about weight distribution and wind direction. Head into a strong wind and it would go airborne. I had done a few 'wheelies' that were rather scary, including one that was so scary, my tackle boxes and fuel tank jumped overboard.

With that background, the story begins on the first day of spring break. I had taken some time off to spend with the boys. Lots of promises to go fishing. That morning, there was terrible weather, thunderstorms with tons of rain. A look at the weather on TV, not good. A cold front is coming. Sorry boys. But Dad, you promised ! Now comes the mistake.

We will go if there is a clearing of the weather. A couple of hours later, a break in the weather. Let's go!!! That voice is still yelling at me. Dad gives in, but only after making it clear that in the event of weather conditions deteriorating, Dad gets to call the trip off without any argument.

We arrived at the Trinity river and a short way up river, a bayou on the right takes you to Lake Charlotte after about a mile or so. This bayou is narrow, about two boat widths, but it is fairly deep, so the trip is quite quick in our race boat.

The first real obstacle is at the entrance to the lake. Very shallow,only inches of water and below that, several feet of mud that is like glue. The trick here was to go as fast as possible and slide all the way to a point where the boat would float again. I had seen several larger boats that were 'unaware' and got stuck and then spent the rest of their day trying to get out.

I would feel sorry for them but there was nothing you could do to help. You could not paddle to them and you couldn't wade either.

Lake Charlotte is a natural lake that is very shallow, about 5 ft on average (this is important). It is about two miles across. We entered the lake at the Southwest corner (also important) and head East along the Cypress trees on the South side. There is no shore. Just Cypress trees standing in the water. About a quarter of a mile, there is a small gap in the Cypress trees that allows you to head south through the Cypress swamp. This was the only path that would allow you access to Mud Lake. The path itself was quite serpentine., any wrong turn and you would 'High Center' on on a Cypress knee.

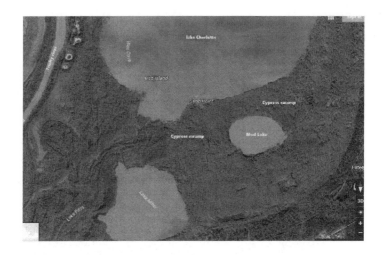

All other paths were blocked with Cypress 'Knees' that were there to ruin any boat. Many lurked just below the surface. A Cypress knee is like a fence post only much harder, more like a steel fence post.

After a few hundred yards of snaking thru the Cypress trees, we come to Mud Lake. Mud is a misnomer, The lake itself has that black clear water that is rarely seen. It is a natural lake also, therefore being quite shallow. A small lake about 200 yards wide. For a number of years, I was the only one that fished there. In the early years, it was much more like catching rather than fishing. More often than not, 40 to 50 fat Bass were caught per trip.

As we emerge from the trees, two things are apparent. The first is the Bass are feeding. Water swirls around the base of a number of Cypress trees. Fairly common when there is a barometer change coming. The second observation was that the weather was going downhill fast. A quick reminder to the boys that it was MY call.

Maybe ten minutes of fishing and the rain starts, big drops. I look to the left and at the base of this tree is a huge boil of the water. Before I could retrieve my lure, Michael drops a spinner bait right on target and there is a huge explosion of water.

A good hook set and the fight is on. I got a good look at the fish on one of its runs past the boat and I surely wished it was on my line. By this time in their lives, both boys were very capable fishermen. Michael handled the fish well, never applying too much pressure. Once in the boat, it was easy to see it was a real 'Trophy' fish.

Alas, here comes more rain. Have to go boys. No arguments UH OH , wind shift out of the North now, the cold front has arrived. Blowing hard now. Remember, we are now headed North back to Lake Charlotte. Proceeding slowly through the trees, bang, what was that? My right hand hurt and a knuckle was bleeding. What? Another bang.

I saw it this time, a hail stone the size of a quarter. Then lots of them. Jeff empties the cooler and now has a nice helmet. Michael, fashions football gear from a life jacket. I am trying to pilot the vessel with the best gear of all, a baseball cap.

Did you ever wonder what it would feel like getting hit on the top of your head with a large hail stone traveling at terminal velocity? It is almost as bad as being hit with one on the top of your shoulder bone.

The hail subsided fairly quickly only to let me see the real trouble coming. Remember I said how shallow the lake was? There was big swells in the water, well back in the trees. Getting closer to the lake, SURF! BIG Surf!

I tried to get out into the lake, but between swells, we would bottom out on the Cypress knees with a huge thud. Engine stops! Can't go back.

We are pinned sideways by the wind against two trees. Not good. The beat down goes on. So we are stuck, holding onto the trees for dear life. Sure is a lot of water in the boat. Crap, the Cypress knees have broken my ship.

Finally catch a break and the wind lets up and so does the surf. We have to get out of here now! The motor starts. Things are looking better. All 25 hp are needed to get this sinking ship moving. Full power, water going out **over** the transom. Drain plug out, were gaining speed and the water level is receding. WOO HOO.

The boat gets up on plane which is mandatory to get across the mud flats. It's working, by the time we hit the shallows, we're doing 40mph. No putting the plug back in, every rivet in the boat looks like a water fountain. There are a few large buckles and bends in the hull also. Those Cypress knees are tough.

We must have been a sight, flying down that bayou. It was funny, because a couple of the rivet fountains were squirting high enough and we were traveling fast enough that the fountain streams were landing in the water behind the boat.

The biggest problems I had now was that it was COLD and I was WET and we were going FAST. The boys were huddled up the best they could. I was not concerned about them, because this was all their fault.

When we approached the boat launch, I told the boys to 'Hang On' because we were going pretty fast when we hit the beach. We finished high and (not so) dry.

Back home, the boys ran straight for the hot showers. There I am being 'Dad' again, I had everything taken care of by the time the boys showed up. Michael asked , "Where's my Fish"? I told him it was in the freezer. What? Where else would it be? I had just finished cleaning it. Did you weigh it Dad? **No**. Did you take a photo Dad? **No**. We could take a photo of the meat though.   **DAD** !!!!

Sorry about that, I should have had it mounted for you, it really was a '**Keeper**'.

The boat was repaired **sort of**. The hull was beat back into shape, **sort of**. Almost every rivet was fiber glassed, **sort of**. The boat from that day on was forever known as 'The Leaky Teaky'

I believe it was a **Coming of Age** moment for my Boys. They will never forget that day.

I hope they never let their kids talk them into poor choices.

Chapter 36

Golf

Golf for me began on the farm. I would get one of my fathers clubs and just start knocking a ball around the farm. On a rare occasion, I would actually hit one correctly and as it flew off, never to be found, I would stare in amazement wondering how I did that. The normal shot would land, if it ever got airborne at all, just a short distance away. I kept hacking and the pure hits became more frequent.

My good hits had a great curve to them. My Dad showed me how to watch my swing path. My swing path was terrible. It went from way outside to way inside when it crossed the ball location. He taught me in five minutes to watch the club cross from inside to outside. I hit my first draw EVER ! (meaning a flight path of right to left) Thanks dad.

My first set of clubs was a set of Wilson 'Blade' irons and Sam Snead woods that my dad bought me.. 'Blade' irons are the hardest irons to hit that have ever been invented. I could not believe they were the choice style for the Pro golfers. Late in life, I purchased a set of Ping I-3s. Incredible difference. My handicap went from 16 to a 9.

Once retired, I moved to Cape Royale on Lake Livingston. I could back my Golf cart out of the garage and be on #1 tee in 5 minutes. Mondays would be 27 holes with friends. Wednesday was men's golf assoc. day so that meant 9 holes to warm up, a 18 hole tournament and 9 more holes of wagering. Friday, 27 more holes. Then, the occasional weekend tournament.

Good Things

There were only a couple of Seniors at the Cape that could give me a game, so on the Club Championship days, I always played in the regular Men's division. I always finished very high, but never won.

159

I have had two "Holes in One". The first I saw all the way. It landed on the green, took one hop, bit and started to roll, taking the slope of the green to the left and dropped in. It felt like I had received a tremendous shock of electricity. I still see it.

The second Hole in One was much less dramatic. I hit a shot that was 'Pure' and I said 'Be Right'. The ball came down and was gone. It was easy to see, the ball flight was right on line. The green was visible with a pin cut in the front. The green was very deep so I knew I could not have 'Flown' the green. On several occasions, I had 'flown' a ball directly in the cup and it was usually followed by a loud 'Clack' and then the sight of the ball being ejected from the hole to land who knows where. I rejected that possibility. Maybe I was fooled and the ball had plugged short barely across a water hazard. The search began and a friend walked to the cup, looked down and asked what type of ball I had hit? He just pointed and said, **'Thar she be Matey'**. What made this one cool was that it was on tournament day and there was a progressive pot that built up until there was an official hole in one. Word spread around the course. People waving from three fairways away. Everyone was waiting at the clubhouse. The 'Bar' tab consumed all my winnings and I had to pay the club an additional $26.00. **It was worth it.**

I played Pinehurst #2 and Pebble beach among the more well known courses. Both brought my ego back where it belonged.

Spanish Bay

A personal favorite was Spanish Bay in Monterey, California. It was so pure, you felt guilty taking a divot.

160

I still have a small (hotel size) whiskey bottle that is full of sand from a trap on the 18th hole at Pebble Beach.

I was fortunate to be at Cherry Hills the year Jack Nicklaus won the U.S. Open. I was in awe.

I played in the World Amateur Tournament at Myrtle Beach twice. I didn't finish well, but it was quite an experience.

My best official score ever (Tournament Play) was a 67. I have the attested card for you 'Nay sayers.'

A Round that is forever!

There was a day that does not count except by me. It was Christmas day and we were going to Houston for a family Christmas. That gathering was not going to be until late afternoon. Jump in the Cart and head off to play a few holes while cooking is going on. Nobody at the course. Club house is locked. Parking lot empty. Oh well, 1st hole , beautiful fade over the Dog Leg right. Crisp 8 iron 12 feet. A good putt, BIRDIE.

2nd hole par 5, smoking drive right through the narrows. Crunched 4 iron. 10 Ft putt in the jar for an Eagle. Two more consecutive birdies. The lights go on. Holy Moly, Birdie, Eagle, Birdie, Birdie. 4 Holes, 5 Under?

I am stopping the story here because, there is no proof. I will say, that I played the whole 18 and I did not make 12 pars. There was not a single bogey made that day. I should have said, That's it, No need to play ever again.

I went LOW that day!

Pebble Beach

As my working career was winding down, in one of the trade periodicals, I saw an advertisement for a Laboratory Seminar on automation that was being held in Monterey, California. Woo Hoo, that's for me. I jumped on the phone and started calling other golfing friends from other company locations. Quickly I found we could have a foursome for Pebble Beach. I made out a travel request and took it to my boss. He looked at it and asked if I could get anything good from this seminar. You bet I said. He knew I was headed for early retirement very soon.

He said, "I suppose you'll be playing some golf". Yes Sir, I already have a 'T' time for Pebble Beach. No need to lie. He signed my request and told me to get the hell out of his office. He was a great guy. Thanks Jerry.

Monterey. The first day of the seminar, here comes one of our foursome and he says he had been thinking that Pebble beach is very expensive and so he was backing out. Just Great! They will not let you play without a foursome. Maybe Pebble will have a fourth for us. A once-in-a-lifetime opportunity is going down the drain. Later that day, the other two pull out. I'm thinking about drowning myself in the Pacific.

That evening, there is a cocktail party and I am less than social. A sales guy from Varian corp. comes up to me and said he heard my golf buddies bailed on me. He asked if I was really interested in the Seminar and I said no. Let's play somewhere in the morning, there are a lot of good courses. (I had done a lot of business with them)

The next morning he picks me up at my hotel and heads out the 17 mile Drive on the Monterey peninsula. You gotta be kidding me. We are cruising by Spanish Bay course and I said WOW, that's beautiful. He said we should play that tomorrow. **Okay!** Not long later, we turn left into **Pebble Beach.**

I look at him and he says I am to swear to never mention this to the 'Drop-outs'. No Problem. He had two other friends waiting for us. I thought for sure I was going to have to listen to sales talk all day. Not One word of shop talk was spoken the whole day. So for Steve and John, my golf bail out guys, if you are reading this, That's what I was doing that day when you couldn't find me. **I was playing Pebble Beach for FREE! NYAH NYAH !**

Memories of Pebble

When we arrived, I went in the clubhouse because I wanted a Pebble Beach logo golf ball. (I collect them) Twelve bucks. Umm no thanks.

Playing the first hole, I hit a pretty good drive in the fairway close to the left rough. I walked over to my ball and then into the rough waiting on another player to hit his second. I looked at the rough and there at my feet, nestled nicely in the rough was a golf ball. It turned out to be a Twelve Dollar golf Ball. I still have it.

At Pebble Beach, you have to have a golf cart and a Caddie. One caddie per foursome. His primary job is to make sure the golf carts stay on the cart paths. They will help with yardage and reading the greens. I asked our caddie if he got some real characters and he just smiled. He said his favorites were the real hackers that asked for yardage when they were a half mile from a green. He said sometimes those guys would ask if they could reach a green in the next county with a three wood. He said the standard reply was, "EVENTUALLY" Ha Ha.

#7 hole, a very short downhill par 3. BIRDIE! Pretty much my highlight reel.

Because of some kind Sales people, it came to pass that I played **Pebble Beach** AND **Spanish Bay** for FREE.

Seventeen Mile drive on the Monterey peninsula is Very beautiful. When you get way out on the point, there is an island. It is known as 'Seal Island' because it is wall to wall seals. Quite amazing, lots of tourists taking photos, myself included. Then, came a wind shift. Remember the story about the Chicken Hatchery and the terrible smell of the egg dump? This came close. In a manor of seconds, the observation area was void of tourists.

One Funny

The guys from Ransomville that I played golf with were a fun bunch. We shared many laughs together and there were quite a few pranks.

This was my best 'Prank'.

Every time I bought a dozen new golf balls, I would carefully save the box and the four sleeves the balls were in.

Through the year of golf, I saved every cut or damaged ball I could find. It was a pretty ugly sight by that winter. At Christmas time, I packaged all of these balls into the packaging I had saved. Not being completely heartless, I did place one brand new ball in each dozen box. Each box was wrapped in festive Christmas wrap with a pretty Bow.

On Christmas Eve, at a fashionably late hour, I drove to each of my friends homes and handed them a special Christmas gift. Each of them felt like crap because they had nothing for me. They begged me to come in for a drink or something. I would beg off because I had more stops to make.

During our doorway conversations, I could observe them handling their gift enough to know that I had bought them a dozen golf balls. I had a hard time controlling my laughter.

~3am on Christmas morning, my doorbell rings followed by the noise of a car speeding off. What? I open the front door and there stood a gift wrapped tube about 2 feet tall and 4 inches in diameter. What? I opened it to find a Seven Iron. The club's shaft had bends that made it look more like a Bugle than a golf club. A good laugh. Thanks for that memory Clyde.

One Last Thing

If you watch golf on TV, you no doubt have heard the announcers say, "He is seeing the line today." Okay, a figure of speech right? **WRONG,** there is such a line.

When I was playing the best golf of my life, I was playing a game with my usual friends when it happened. I was on the first green, pin high about 15' left of the pin. I started to line up my putt and there it was. It looked like someone had a small paint roller, maybe 2" wide. There was a pale green stripe from my ball all the way to the hole. It looked almost neon on the dark green grass.

It actually scared me. I blinked a couple of times and it was still there, curving slightly right showing me a two cup break. I knew instantly that if I could start the ball on that line, it would be pure. After calming down for a second, I backed off and told the guys they were in serious trouble. Lots of chuckles, snickers etc. I stepped up and calmly rolled in a putt that was as pure as they come.

I saw it several times that day and each time I saw it and started the putt on the line, it was a sure thing. Holes where I didn't see it, I would stall waiting for it. That did not work.

We finished the round, I collected my winnings and headed for the Pro Shop. I found the Pro and told him I had actually SEEN the line on the greens. He asked what I saw? I told him thinking I would get a good laugh.

He said 'Yep, I have seen it when I was a tour wannabe'. He said he quit seeing it and played right into a club Pro job. He said he knew pro's that said they saw it every day. For me, there was only one more occasion that I saw it. Sounds crazy I know, but it's what I saw.

I am no artist But it looked something like this

Chapter 35

Herb

Herb came into my life in the Technical department of duPont. Herb was,...A Character.

I remember he transferred to Texas from an East Coast facility. Our office building had quite high windows, so you had to stand up to see out. This one morning, about 9am, I was in an office talking to a friend. I happened to look out at the parking lot across the street and there is Herb sneaking through the parking lot. Way late for work on like his second day. Quickly I ran door to door telling everyone about the show. Every time he made a stealthy move, a cheer would go up. He swore up & down that he was not sneaking anywhere.

Not long after that, We needed a forth for our Golf game. A friend said that he heard that Herb played golf. Not sure if this will work. The other three of us were free spirits, if you will. Herb was a tad stuffy. He played with us on a regular basis and we got him to loosen up a bit.

Herb learned that I went to Colorado Trout fishing every year. He was soon bragging about his Trout fishing on the Raritan river in New Jersey. The Raritan River? New Jersey? I think he was catching Coney Island Whitefish.

I finally gave in and told him okay for one trip to Colorado. I knew from talking to him, 250 miles in one day was big. I on the other hand was thinking a thousand miles at a time. I asked, do you have tents, sleeping bags etc. Answer, No, we're staying in a Condo. What? Major mistake, I said okay.

The plan, Herb and his wife would leave on a certain date. We would leave Three days later and meet them in Albuquerque NM. All arriving the same day.

Mistake #2. I told Herb that when he came down from the Sandia mountains on I-40, take the very first exit in the city of Albuquerque. On the right , the first Motel is where we will stay. I think it's a Super 8 or something. Just stay there, we will be later than you..

We arrive and it's a Days Inn. Oh well, where the hell is Herb? He must be running way late. Herb is usually holed up by 1pm? We drive up and down the highway cruising every parking lot. No Herb. We are about to turn in when I have a scary thought. You don't suppose?

I grab a phone book and I see there is a Super 8 motel but it is outside the city on I-25 North. Pull around back of the Super 8 and there is Herb's van. I truly wanted to let the air out of all his tires. Bang on the door and wake him up. He says What, you said the Super 8. I look and there on the table is the notes I left for him. Read this to me Herb. **TAKE THE FIRST EXIT, THE FIRST MOTEL IS A SUPER-8 I THINK. JUST STAY THERE, WE WILL BE LATER THAN YOU.**

Now, this is an educated man. He held a Masters degree in Chemical Engineering. I said too bad they didn't have a common sense class.

The next morning, we meet up at the now infamous Super 8 and head off for Durango. Next problem is Herbs old Toyota van does 40 mph up hill and maybe 60 down hill. Try following that for a while.

Arriving in Durango finally, just time for a quick late lunch then it's off to condo camping. Hey there's a McDonald's. Quick and fast. We go inside , Herb does not do drive through at all. It is readily apparent Herb is flumixed by the clown that greets him even though it's a plastic clown. No waitress?

No Just give the kid your order at the Counter. Okay, Herb says, " I would like a burger, medium rare on Rye please. Where is the wine menu? This is going to be a long trip.

We get to the condo and his wife says they had better stay downstairs because Herb snores. He snores? No, they both SNORE! LOUD! It was like music from Deliverance only it was played on dueling Uvulas instead of a Banjo and Guitar. It was awful.

167

The Fishing Begins

For months, I had to listen to Herb jawing about this awesome split Bamboo fly rod he had. He made it sound like it would guide you to the fish. Whoever had his hands on the that Fly Rod was just along for the ride.

A short ride from the Condo to a stream that always held a fair number of 'Stocker' trout. Herb breaks out the trout slayer. This I have to get my hands on. I have used bamboo fly rods numerous times and have never rated one above fair. Fly rods are rated (at least by me) as to how much 'Backbone' it has with the minimum of weight. Herb's 'Trout Slayer' had the 'backbone' of a Jellyfish.

Never one to be very diplomatic, I asked if he could cast a fly further than his shadow and burst out laughing. This did not set well with Herb.

I just couldn't watch. He would whip that rod back and forth like he was losing control of the lions in a Circus. Back and forth, probably three whips per second.

At one point, when he would slow down enough, I noticed his Fly was missing, no doubt popped off with the sonic crack of the whip. These flies were easy to see, they were quite large being a stimulater pattern. Not wanting to be chastised again, I kept quiet and Herb fished on for 15 minutes whipping that stream into submission without a fly. Hey, my fly is gone. No S___ !

How bad did he whip that river? He was taking twenty strokes to my one and about 30 feet was his max distance.

The next day I told Herb we would go remote to a place that had hundreds of trout. This was met with numerous snide remarks.

The following morning, we boarded a shuttle train that used the narrow gauge rails for the D&SRR (Durango & Silverton steam train). The neat part was they made several stops along the way where hikers and fishermen could get off along the Animas river. We rode up to Cascade Junction where we were going to fish.

Right away Herb looks at the Animas River and says Oh Boy. I said wait, you don't want to fish here, there are too many minerals and who knows what coming down from the mines upstream at Silverton. I said we we had to cross the river on a suspension bridge that was here for Horses and Hikers. Then, we would fish Cascade creek that came down a canyon from the West.

Herb, "Nope, I'm fishing right here. This looks perfect". What a knucklehead. So we said bye and said we would be back in time to catch the 4pm shuttle train.

Cascade creek was awesome. Virtually every place there was no rapids, you could see really good Rainbow trout that were waiting for us. We hammered them and probably caught a hundred. That does not happen often. What a day.

We got back around three to find Herb sitting under a tree. How did you do I asked. Herb said he did great. He landed three fish and he said he had them right there in his cooler. Being polite, he asked how we did. I said probably closer to three hundred. This didn't set well. "Oh yeah, Where are they?" Catch & release dude! Bull S___, was his reply.

Several days later, we went back and I made Herb fish Cascade creek. He talked about that day until he died. I will not say how many fish we caught, because you would say I am just another lying fisherman. I will say that we brought home fish that were injured and did not look like they would survive. There were Fifteen Rainbow trout in our cooler.

Saving Herb $200

One of the most amazing places to fish in the United States is the San Juan river in New Mexico. It is just South of Durango Colorado. It is in the 'High' desert which means you may be burning up in the heat of the Sun and loose all feeling in your feet because the water temperature is a brisk 40 degrees f.

For several miles below the Navajo Dam, there is a fishery unequaled anywhere I have ever fished. It is difficult fishing for several reasons.

The first is the food that the trout feed on. The food is the Midge fly. The adult midge is maybe 1/8 inch long. There is the big problem, a fly that replicates an emerging midge is tiny. Usually a size 20 to 24 hook. You have to have some good magnification to tie that onto 7X tippet material.

Next problem is the Strike. The fish of the San Juan are a hybrid variety known as "Cut Bows". This is a cross between a Cutthroat trout and a Rainbow trout. To some, they are called Rocket rainbows due to what happens when they feel the sting of a hook. The average fish is 3 pounds.

A fact of nature is that a fish can not expend more energy to catch food than the food value of its catch. So the presentation of this tiny fly is critical. It has to be drifting at the depth required for the trout to see it. The trout will see it just before it drifts to the fish. A strike is the fish simply opens its mouth and closes it once the midge has entered. If you are waiting for a tap or a swirl, you will catch nothing there.

Attached to your leader material, you have a small piece of yarn that floats on the surface. A strike is nearly invisible, just a slight twitch of the yarn. A quick flick of the fly rod down stream will quickly let you know if it was indeed a strike.

Remember the term 'Rocket Rainbow'. I have had some that stripped off all my fly line and backing line, then the ping of the tippet material breaking and the trout is still going. Re-rig and start again. Once, I did a hook set but didn't think it was a fish. I found out it was. It was a fish that departed so fast, the fly line burned a nasty cut in my index finger.

Kind of got technical there. Back to the story of saving Herb cash. We had just started a day of fishing on the San Juan. We had been fishing maybe 15 minutes when I hear this splash, splash, splash coming behind me. Turning, I see Herb coming up the flats we were fishing dragging a big loop of fly line in the river. What? Herb says, we have to go. Why? Herb says , I hooked myself. What? Where?

He turns his head to the side and there on the side of his jaw is a Chocolate colored midge emerger, size20 with a small patch of white simulating wings.

Once I stopped laughing, I said well pull it out dummy. You always fish with barbless hooks at the San Juan. He says he can't because this fly has a BARB. What? I take out my clippers and free the line from the Dummy. How does that feel Herb? He says he cant feel it now that the line is off.

Great I said, I'm going back fishing now. So we fished the rest of the day. I just couldn't look at him. Too Funny !

Walking back to the car, Herb asks where the Hospital is in Durango. What for, I'll remove the fly. I have done it before and the patient survived. No way are you cutting on me he says. Trust me I say with a snicker. We have a couple of beers and head off to Durango and the Hospital.

How much is the emergency room fee? Probably $200 or more. Have another beer Herb. A while later, he says, you think you can take it out? Sure, have a beer. We get to Durango, a bit slurred, 'you certain you can take the fly out?' Sure, have another can of anesthesia.

Forget the ER, Back to the condo. Herb busts through the door saying, "I hooked myself, but Bob is going to save me $200".

Tensions are increasing by the second with Herb's wife. I decide to play it up a bit. I return from the kitchen with a butcher's knife, slashing it back and forth on a sharpening stone. She doesn't look so good. Suzanne explains that I know what I'm doing because I cut one out of her leg before. Herb is fine, enjoying yet another cool beverage.

His wife is a lost cause now so I decide I better back off. I said I was just kidding and put the butcher's knife back. I returned with my small pocket knife and resumed the sharpening. I said okay Herb, sit right here on this bar stool. (how appropriate) I examine the surgical patient and proclaim that I doubt we will need sutures. She says wait! That knife should be sterile. What? It's fine, I wiped it on my pants we are good to go. Herb, would you like a wooden spoon to bite on? Herb? Earth to Herb, come in? He's ready for brain surgery.

Uh oh, I'm losing her again. The Patient is nearly Comatose. I give in, Hey, pour me a shot of that Jack Daniels. She thinks that is a great idea. The first idea she likes. She pours the Jack and hands it to me knowing I am about to sterilize my knife with the World's finest Bourbon. Holding my knife over the Jack, I hesitate, tilt my head and throw back the Jack. Okay, here we go.

Herb mumbles an incoherent something. One tiny nick and there is the size 20 **Barbed** chocolate emerger in my hand, slightly discolored with dried blood.

When Herb's wife came to, she examined the wound and admitted that I did a good job. Herb thinks he remembered.

Losing my Friend

After the previous story, we had other fishing trips. When I started working in Yellowstone, Herb would come every summer for a week to fish with me. We had a favorite wilderness spot to fish that was a fairly strenuous hike of three miles to get to it. I am sitting here typing this and I am looking at a 8x10 glossy Of that spot with Herb and I each holding a nice Yellowstone Cutthroat.

The point is made to set what happened in 1999. Herb arrived in Yellowstone that year and we went fishing.

A Double with my Friend Herb

The first place we fished was easy. Maybe a 200yd walk and it was flat. On the way out, he had to stop and rest. Holy crap Herb, you are in terrible shape. You need to exercise more.

There was no way he was going to make the three mile one way trek in the wilderness to our favorite spot that year.

We said goodbye and they left for Idaho so Herb could fish the Lochsa river. His favorite place ever. The Lochsa and Salmon rivers join there and become the Clearwater fork of the Snake River.

A day later, his wife calls and said Herb is gone. What? Where did he go? She said he was fishing the Lochsa and when he came home he said he didn't feel good. She said he didn't look good to her either. So Herb lays down for a nap in the RV. She heads for the campground host to find a nearby clinic. Returning to the RV, Herb has gone to meet the great Fisher of Men. I can think of a lot of worse ways to go.

She had no clue about driving an RV and there was none in their family that did either so it was off to Idaho and from there to Texas for me. Herb's wife said she wanted to ride with me to Texas. I told her we were going to do more than 250 miles a day. She said okay if I could just get her and their RV back to Texas.

She had no idea their RV was that fast. Idaho to Galveston in three days with a truck and a 38 foot RV.   Whee!

I still have that #20 Chocolate emerger with a Barb.

Herb, you were a Dork, but I miss you.

P.S. After our first trip to Colorado, Herb retired the 'Bamboo Wonder' and became an Orvis guy. (Baby Got Backbone) He never would admit that it is hard to cast with a NOODLE.

Chapter 38

Yellowstone National Park

Yellowstone National Park remains one of my favorite memories. Friends made, The Fishing, Guiding, Hiking, all of it.

That era begins not long after I retired from duPont at the end of '93. We spent most of '94 rebuilding our lake cabin on Lake Livingston into a permanent home.

In '95 we hooked up our RV and headed for the mountain states. We spent a lot of time in Colorado, Montana, Alberta, British Columbia, Idaho and Wyoming.

Our way home brought us through Yellowstone in October and the weather was perfect. There were no crowds like they said would ruin our visit.

We wanted to see Old Faithful of course. No problem, drive over to it, sit down in the front row with six other people and watch the show. It was like that everywhere we went. Awesome! At one point, we stopped at a store in the park for the traditional tourist treasures. I was buying some trout flies to replenish my supply and this older sales guy strikes up a conversation. I asked how he got a job like that? Without a word, he reached under the counter and handed me a card.

Job Opportunities in Yellowstone.

He said that some 70% of the employees are retired folks just like me. 20% are college student/faculty and 10% are those that just 'hang-out' meaning they work parks in the summer and Ski areas in winter. ie: career under achievers. He also said every National Park is looking for people like me. He said, they have RV places for workers or Dorm rooms.

My head is wrapped around this. I can sell Trout flies for sure. All the way back to Texas, I'm thinking about selling flies.

Back in Texas, where to begin? Secretary of the interior, where else. Off goes a letter with a Bio. I said we wanted to work in the inter-mountain region. Gosh, where would I like to work? First choice, Glacier National Park. No doubt, It is awesome.

Time passes (5 days). A letter from the Secretary of the Interior with addresses and contacts for the National Parks and private vendors. They, also had passed on my Bio. More time passes, (5 more days). Hey three large packets of info from three of the parks. Cool, fill out the applications and back in the mail. Wow, fast. The next day, postman at my door.

What? Another half dozen packets. The day after, a note in my mail box. "please come to the Post Office to pick up your mail." So much for R.F.D.

Next the offers. The first from Grand Canyon National park wanted to know if I would come for the summer to do "Trail Maintenance"? Simple, you take a pack of mules down into the canyon fixing wash-outs, removing fallen trees, fallen rocks , just about anything that was not proper, and BTW , you might be rough camping as long as ten days at a time. Um, if I look at a horse funny, I'm the one that gets hurt first. Mules? MULES? That equals Death wish. Turned that one down.

Did you know that all the parks are looking for workers to clean Pit Toilets? One of the higher paying jobs. And so it went, lot's of job offers , but none from Glacier. Yellowstone called and said they would love to have us and they gave us choices. We decided to accept jobs in a "Small" store on Lake Yellowstone. Over 9,000 ft of altitude. Takes some getting used to.

The contracts are express delivered to us, signed and returned. Please report on June the 1st. WooHoo.

About 10 days before leaving for Yellowstone, a phone call, It's Glacier National Park. Too late! It's because they are the last of the National Parks to open. I asked if they always are late calling? Yep. I'm thinking they must get some high quality workers.

Bridge Bay Marina

On May 31st, we arrived at the South entrance to the park where a Ranger told us we were lucky because they had only opened the South entrance the day before.

Had it still been closed, it was another 400 miles around to Idaho Falls to come in from the West..

There was not a lot to see except for walls of snow that were higher than our RV. Another view was that of Bison butts as they wandered along the road ahead of us. They had no clue about keep right laws. SLOW!

June 1st, we check in for our job briefings, paper work etc. We Meet Pat & Keith that we would be working with. We are still friends today. We had a lot of fun with them hiking and fishing.

Their RV, contained a small Zoo. One I remember was a cat named moocher or Moochie. Who travels with a Cat? The featured attraction was a big African Grey Parrot. Keith had taught it some Juicy words. When they walked the cat, the parrot would say, "There goes that Damn Cat again".

The store at Bridge Bay was quite small. Smaller than a typical 7-11. On arrival, there was not much to see, just a mountain of boxes out front. Lots of work to do. The store opens in a few days and fishing season opens on June 15. What? Lake Yellowstone is frozen solid. The same for the Marina. The docks are heaved up on the Ice. 10 days later, no Ice anywhere. Amazing.

Day one, we are busy busy opening boxes, stocking shelves etc. The store manager asks me to step into his office. What have I done? He asks if I would be the fishing and camping department manager. Umm, I guess so.

Hey, guess what, it hasn't been two hours and I have been promoted. A true rising star. Almost lunch time, I get a request to visit the managers office. I knew it, they made a terrible mistake, my 10 cent raise is down the drain.

Surprise, the question is would I be a shift supervisor? Umm, okay. Off to lunch I'm a big wheel now. Ha. That afternoon, another office visit, They need an assistant manager. Umm, okay. Three promotions in one day, is that a record?

A month later, the manager asks me talk to him. He says there is a store manager position open for a bigger store that is open year around and he wants it. The company said they would love to have him, but there was nobody to take over the Marina Store. He told them he had just the guy they needed to take over. Umm, Okay.

So the cycle was complete, mop boy to top management in less than two months. Things happen quickly there.

When we were setting up the store, I made an interesting observation. Someone had gone crazy when ordering fishing lures. One lure in particular.

It was called a Jake's Lure. Looked a lot like a tie clip and it had one treble hook. The predominate color was Gold with small red dots. 12 to a box and there was dozens and dozens of boxes.

A whole section of the store room was taken up Just for Jake's lures. You gotta be kidding. No, not at all, we ran out on several occasions. I wish I would have saved my order catalog that also kept track of sales. We sold **thousands** of them.

Otters playing on the docks, Osprey building a nest across the bay. Just beautiful. Here come the People. **LOTS** of People. Opening day of fishing season was crazy. A huge line just to get a fishing license. To give you some idea, at this little 'Mom & Pop' sized store, we would take in revenues of $250,000 in four months time.

Where to fish?

By mid summer, I had a few really hot fishing spots. People were coming into the store all the time complaining that everywhere they stopped to fish, there were no fish. I would explain that 95% of the fisherman would stop at those awesome looking spots along the road. Simple , the fish quickly learned that was where those sharp fishing hooks were at also.

Well then, where are they? They are in the hard to find places. Where is that at? That is why you need a guide.. Where can I find a guide? You're talking to one. Really? How much? $150 a day guaranteed. Guaranteed? Yep, I will get you hooked up on 15" trout, many of them. How many you land is up to your ability. No catch, no Pay, simple. I never had a customer that did not pay. The norm was a nice tip would be included. I had customers that easily caught 100 trout in a day. What was surprising to me was that I had set a rule for everyone I took into the 'Back' country. It was simple, They had to pack out all of their trash plus ONE more piece of trash. They all thought that was a great idea. Some times, it was difficult. They might only find a cigarette filter.

All this was possible because I was the store manager and I could adjust my schedule.

I really enjoyed guiding beginners because they had no bad habits. A 'fisherman' that rated himself as 'good' was impossible to coach.

Knowing that you have purchased my book, if you are going to Yellowstone and are planning on fishing, contact me, theflycaster at yahoo and I will put you onto the most incredible 'fishing hole' ever.

The Flycaster

I have been asked many times about my nickname 'the Flycaster'. Ranger Rick the head Lake Ranger dropped that on me. I would see him often either in the store or out on the lake or streams. We got to be pretty good friends. One day he came in the store and when he saw me he said, "Hey, it's The Fly Caster". My friend Roy heard it and so I became Theflycaster. I certainly have been called worse.

Returning

At the end of the first season, I was asked if I would come back as the 'Full time' manager of Bridge Bay Marina. And so the adventure continued through the summers of 1996, 97, 98 & 99.

Photo Op

Our company, park wide, sold thousands of Post cards. None of them had a decent photo of a Yellowstone Cutthroat Trout. It became my mission to fix that. The Photo below is now for sale at Yellowstone with my photo credit on the back.

The only Photo I ever sold !
It's now a Post Card in the Stores
at Yellowstone N.P.

It is still for sale in Yellowstone N.P. Photo Credit on the back.

178

After our first year in Yellowstone, We were asked to come a month early to help with store openings at other locations. We were prime employees to do that because our store was one of the last to open. It was fun. And I had my own vehicle.

Madison River

My Company Van

Arriving for work at Yellowstone on May the First, had pluses and minuses. The best part was that there were no tourists. The bears were near the roads and they were easy to spot in the snow.

The bad part was the Buffalo were on the roads, going somewhere. There were times when you would look at the same Buffalo butts for a long way. There was one guy from the company would actually bump them to get them out of the way. That is like WAY illegal. We could still get around quite easily with the park being closed to tourists.

Did I mention that a thermometer would still be reading nothing on the first of May?

The other bad part was we had to drive all the way to Idaho to enter the park from the West. It is a long drive from Texas.

In the HR department, they have a big map of the United States. When you arrive for work, they give you a color coded pin. A different color showing the number of years of service. You would then put the pin on the map on your home. There were pins in every State and city. One year I thought I would do my home town the honor of getting pinned. Amazing, there was already a pin in Ransomville NY. I saw two pins in Wilson NY. Very Cool.

Our third year, we were asked to come the first of May and stay until the end October for store closings. Bitter cold to start and bitter cold when we left.

Our fourth year, they asked us to come on APRIL fools day and stay until the end of October. This because Suzanne got a job as assistant to the Jewelry buyer. She ended up not liking that position because she drove somewhere in the park every day. That is a lot of traffic jams.

During the pre season, I worked with two guys that were really great. Chip was the Camping and Recreation department buyer and was married to one of the company owners. A really cool guy. Garland, was from Texas and was an assistant to Chip.

All through the summer he would drive the Park visiting all the stores. On occasion, he would deliver a rush order to me from the warehouse. Usually fishing lures that we were always running out of. I traveled the park a lot with Garland doing store openings and closings.

A short story about Garland. The first year I worked at Yellowstone I was shocked to see the Great White Pelicans floating on the Yellowstone river when everything but the river was frozen. I was also shocked to see the numbers of big trout these birds were gulping down.

The Pelicans are plentiful in Corpus Christi during the winter. I never did know where they went in the summer.

So here I am riding with Garland along the Upper Yellowstone river and I could see the Pelicans feeding at the Hardy rapids. The migrating fish get bottle necked there and so it is easy pickings for the pelicans. One after another. down the throat.

I mentioned to Garland that the Pelicans were a great surprise to see in the winter time. Remember it is winter in Yellowstone until early June. Garland says, " me too, the first time I saw them, I looked them up at the Library." This I will never forget.

Garland says,"Yep, those White Pelicans are MAGNATORY." Yes I spelled it correctly. MAGNATORY.

Garland, you still make me smile.

Gus

At the beginning of the 1999 season, we were staying at a company owned RV park in West Yellowstone Montana. It is a very big RV park and we had it pretty much to ourselves. It was before tourist season and most of the RV spaces were well hidden by snow. Our space had to be cleared with a big 'Front-End' loader and there was still a lot of shovel work to find the Electric meter, water and sewer connections.

We (Suzanne actually) had a Min-pin named Dolly. Such a fun dog. She was allowed to run free because the tourists were not yet arriving. That dog could run like the wind and she loved the snow.

One day my friend Roy had come by to visit. We were sitting outside when we saw Dolly running on the street heading for home. Nothing unusual about that until she got right to the RV. She jumped a small puddle and collapsed right at my feet. She died within 30 minutes.

Later we heard from a Veterinarian that there were other cases just like Dolly. It was found that a snowmobile rental business was having a lot of damage done to their rentals by ravens. Wiring and upholstery damage.

The business owner put out nice things like poisoned turkey carcasses etc. Very illegal to kill anything like that. The problems came to light because the Ravens would carry off the poisoned meat and drop it everywhere. Dogs, cats and all sorts of wildlife paid the ultimate price.

To put it mildly, there was much sadness in our RV. Talk of leaving the park etc. Then Carrie, Suzanne's boss, Told her that she had seen a Min-Pin at the animal shelter in Bozeman, Montana where her home is. A phone call confirmed it. Our next day off found us headed for Bozeman.

The shelter brought out Gus, the 'Min-Pin' for us to meet. Gus looked like a Min-Pin but was substantially bigger. Not the size of a Doberman Pincer, maybe half a Doberman. Suzanne was disappointed. The shelter gave Suzanne a letter that was left by the woman that had surrendered Gus. I was getting to know Gus and I liked him right away, but this was to be Suzanne's choice.

I looked to where Suzanne stood reading the letter and she had tears streaming down her face. I told the girl from the shelter to start the paper work because I was now certain GUS was about to become a TEXAN.

I read the letter also. The woman that gave him up could not afford the $10 surrender fee. This animal shelter is the rare 'No-Kill' type. If not adopted, any animal just stays there the rest of their life.

There was a couple of other things in the letter. Gus hates traveling in a vehicle. He loves children. So the adoption papers are signed and Gus is headed for Yellowstone. Trouble with riding in a car? Not a peep from Gus. Within 5 minutes Gus is sound asleep on Suzanne's lap. He loves my Diesel truck. Kids are fine, but put the same kid on a bicycle or skateboard and Gus was pissed off. It took a while but that issue was resolved.

Later doing research, It proved to be that Gus perfectly met all the standards of a German Pincer. Not a Miniature Pincer, Not a Doberman, he was a **German Pincer**. I didn't know there was such a breed. It seems that the German Pincer breed is much older than the Doberman or Min Pin breeds.

As a side note, every time we went to Bozeman, we would drop off a 50lb bag of food at the Shelter. They are good people.

Back in Texas Gus was in heaven, especially when the deer would come into our yard and that was every day. There was no controlling him then, the chase was on. Lucky for me, he loved my diesel truck more than chasing deer. I would just slowly drive the roads below our property and he would come tearing out of the woods chasing after me. Jump in the truck with the look of, "Where are we going?" Home Gus.

The deer issue was resolved with a picket fence. It didn't stop the Deer or Gus at first. The deer would just hop over and Gus could jump onto the top cross rail then over the top. Next was a 'Hot' wire around the top.

The wiring project was only live for 15 minutes when from in our house, I heard a sharp YELP. From that moment on, the wire was not 'Hot'. For Gus, just seeing the wire was enough. He knew it had teeth.

In a short amount of time, Gus was MY dog and everyone could see it. I had a small lawn tractor and Gus rode on the hood while I mowed.

He liked to run for miles along side my golf cart.

When he was in my truck, nobody, **NOBODY** would reach in that window.

After moving to Corpus Christi, life changed for Gus. No more deer to chase, no golf cart and no lawn tractor. He just had me, my truck and our home to guard.

August 18, 2006, I'm out for a walk with Gus. It is just breaking daylight and at this park, across the street, I see a Doberman coming and it is aggressive. Not a bounding run, it is in a flat out sprint. I thought oh Lord, he intends to kill Gus.

Boy, was I wrong. Twenty feet away, he goes airborne. It's my face he wants. Having played football and other sports, I will tell you that was the hardest hit I have ever received. That dog flipped me and the result was a broken L1 vertebra. My trusty 1 iron saved me from that dog. Lot's of intense pain. I will spare you the rest of that story. I will tell you, I asked God for help that day. I was still **Coming of Age.**

Gus was with me all thru my rehab. At first, he could not understand why It took a half hour to walk to the mail box and back. My strength was returning and we were back to long walks again.

Gus lived until 2012. His grave is under the pine trees at the farm. He loved that place. He was a true friend.

Chapter 39

Yellowstone N.P.

Tales

'Take Hookie Out'

The story I am about to tell is True. I have a Newspaper article to prove it. Well sort of, the Newspaper article is based on a reporter's interview with myself and other employees of Bridge Bay Marina.

It begins with a normal busy morning. Being the store manager, It was the preferred method to 'dump' difficult customers on me. I was summoned to the front and to much joy of the employees, I was given a couple from Japan that spoke Zero English. I escorted them out of harms way (rude tourists). After several bows to each other, I finally determined they wanted to fish. All this was done by hand gestures. More bowing. We were the only store in the park that rented fishing tackle that consisted of a spinning rod, a reel and one lure.

A half hour has passed and the deal is nearly complete. One problem, I am sure, they do not have a fishing license. I show them the License book and through many more hand gestures, the answer is no license.

A full hour has past, and it is time for a half dozen bows from my customers and myself. I escort them out and behind me I hear a lot of

Snicker, snicker, giggle, giggle...I'll get even one day. I hear comments of that's why you make the big bucks Mr. Manager.

No time to issue discipline, we are busy. About an hour passes and I look out the window. Here is the little Japanese fellow walking by, in one hand, his fishing rod in the other hand is a Motor boat rental form from the rental place next door. I said Uh Oh, here comes a shipwreck. I was seriously concerned, because I had grown fond of these visitors.

Back to work, busy. Minutes pass and someone is pulling on my shirt from behind. It's my Japanese friend. More bows, lots of hand gestures.

Finally, in very broken English and hand motions, the words come out, "TAKIE HOOKIE OUT" (That's as close as I can get) I show him we sell forceps and needle nose pliers for that. Pliers it is. Sold. He won't let go of me, "TAKIE HOOKIE OUT, TAKIE HOOKIE OUT!" over and over. He's dragging me out of the store.

At this point let me say that our Marina is full of big trout but fishing is not permitted due to the Hazards of kids around etc.

I get it, he couldn't stand it and he has caught a Trout. If a ranger sees him, he is busted, no exceptions. I decide to help to keep the fella from being fined. I took about a half step outside and nearly did a face plant, because I see it **clearly**.

There she is, the little Japanese bride who never spoke a word standing there with a **TREBLE HOOK THROUGH BOTH LIPS.** I can't be anywhere near this lawsuit. Through both lips? How does that happen? I am saying and pointing Hospital three Kilometers, Hospital three Kilometers.

I break free and run back inside. All the employees have their faces pressed against the glass. There he goes pliers in hand and he goes to work on her. Much blood. The small crowd that had gathering dissipated rapidly. The women inside quickly closed the blinds amid some retching and gagging.

Minutes pass and here comes the little fellow. He wants his money back for the fishing rental. I cheerfully refunded his money even though I noticed my lure was missing. I pointed up the hill and said, "Hospital Three Kilometers" A couple of quick bows and he was off with his bride that had new body piercings.

Later that day, Ranger Rick, the head Lake Ranger came in and asked what happened. He said he was hearing all sorts of versions. He said he was off to the hospital to check it out. The next day he told me they had left the hospital before he got there. Two hooks removed and a shot for infection prevention.

A few days later, I am visited by a reporter and camera man from the West Yellowstone News wanting an interview.

Ah, the price of Fame.

Chapter 40

Yellowstone N.P.

Another Tale

Never Cry Wolf

Since the reintroduction of the Wolf in 1995 to Yellowstone National Park, The Wolf has surpassed the Grizzly bear as the most desired sighting. This tale is about Wolf sightings real or imagined.

The Store I managed was at Bridge Bay Marina on Lake Yellowstone. The store was located on the North shore of Bridge Bay giving us a beautiful view of the Marina and on the opposite side of the bay was a forest of Lodge Pole Pine. Looking to the Southwest, there was a meadow perhaps three to four acres. Several times a week, a Coyote would appear and begin hunting small rodents. Without fail, a tourist would burst into the store exclaiming with much excitement, "There is a WOLF in the meadow"!

For some time, I would look out and then burst a bubble by telling them it was a beautiful animal, but it indeed was a Coyote. Most times, I would get an argument because they were certain that animal was a Wolf.

The closest you could get to the meadow was on the Ranger's dock and you would still be 150 to 200 yards away.

Coyote   Wolf

One day, I thought, why ruin the tourist's hopes. The next Tourist that came in Crying WOLF, I looked out and said, "Do you have any idea of how lucky you are?". Believe me, THIS was **EXACTLY** what they wanted to hear.

Those tourists left Yellowstone with a memory that I am sure was retold hundreds of times. There were also hundreds of those disposable cameras sold in my store so people could get a photo of a Wolf.

Keep in mind, a photo of the Coyote, excuse me, Wolf from that distance with a Kodak disposable camera was about the size of a pepper grain on an 8X10 sheet of paper. I am certain many of those photos were shown countless times with the proud owner proclaiming the dot in the Meadow was a Wolf because a Store Manager there told me how lucky I was.

A friend from Texas came to visit me in the Park. He said there was a Wolf lying right by the road in Hayden Valley. I tried to explain but I gave up and he also left being one Happy Camper. R.I.P. Rudy.

It's all about the Memories you see,

Real OR Imagined.

Chapter 41

ESPANA

I had been giving a lot of thought about my 'Bucket List'. I did not actually have a list, because I have been blessed with a good life. Yet, I was thinking of what I might want to do with the time I have left.

Then, browsing through Netflix, I saw a Martin Sheen movie titled 'The Way'. I watched the movie and I was 'Moved'. WOW, I watched it again. It is a movie about a man who loses his son that had gone to Spain to walk the Camino de Santiago. His son was killed on the first day of his pilgrimage.

The Camino de Santiago is a pilgrimage that starts in France and continues across Northern Spain to Santiago where believers say St James is buried. It is religious to many, but there are hundreds of reasons to do it. Mine was to become a better person and return to a simple life. Many hours spent walking through forests and farmland will give you plenty of time to purge your mind. At night, there is no TV or Radio. It is a good thing.

This Pilgrimage is not for everyone, mountains, long flat areas etc. People have been making this trek since the year 600AD. Many in Europe start the pilgrimage from their home. They trek all the way to Santiago and then return home on the same path. Stockholm Sweden to Santiago Spain and back is a LONG walk.

My research begins. YouTube was a great resource. I started blogging and met a lot of people with much information. It was beginning to consume me. Not long later, I announced to my family that my 'Bucket List' had but one item. It was met with some serious objections, but later after they researched it, there were requests to go with me. In the end, it was just Suzanne and I. Most people that have jobs can not get 5 to 6 weeks off to make the pilgrimage. Thus, the majority of trekkers are retirees or college students.

Training

Only a fool would attempt this trek without training. Everyday, a minimum of four miles of walking. Then it was Four miles everyday with a Pack. Then it was four miles with a heavy pack.

One day, there was trouble, I was carrying a heavy pack and stretched my distance out a lot. I was trekking along the shoreline of Corpus Christi Bay when I began suffering a groin pull. I still had a mile left and I was afraid I would be on my hands and knees. Like magic, there was a park bench. I sat for a while and started to feel a little better. I looked up and across the street, there was a sculpture of Jesus standing in the front of a boat with his arms spread looking right at me. I knew I was going to be okay.

Medical

Part of the preparations was medical insurance. My Medicare means nothing in Europe, so I had to upgrade to premium supplemental insurance. The Zero deductible insurance that would cover 80% of costs while overseas. This proved to be a good thing.

I had to get checkups etc. My first was to a Dermatologist. I had a tiny spot on my neck that would bleed if I scratched it. Yes, I knew what it was. My Doctor says, That looks like skin cancer. What is this spot? Uh oh, let the fun begin. Five Cancers. Three on my neck, one on my cheek, one on my back. A good time to have Zero deductible.

Off for my general physical. Hmm, my prostate is enlarged. Off to see a Urologist. Biopsy time. What fun. A serious relief when I get the word there is **no cancer**. Still, they say the prostate has to be reduced. Zero deductible to the rescue.

Woo Hoo, all successful. Start my training again. Bicycle training. Miles of it. Feeling great now. The effort is worth it. Another set back. It's rush hour, only a fool would ride in the street so I am riding on the sidewalk next to a very busy street. Going by a section of businesses, I look to my left and see a big SUV heading out of a parking lot. The lady driver is looking left, checking for an opening in the traffic.

Unfortunately for me, there was an opening so she guns it. I get broadsided and knocked into the street. I don't remember much other than a lot of pain. I thought my back was broken again. There was someone driving in the opposite lane of traffic that saw me and they swerved across the street and stopped, blocking traffic that might run over me. Thank you, whoever you are. I vaguely remember this woman asking me if she hit me or if I had just fallen off my bike? DUH. I remembered a girl holding my head still. She said she was a Nurse. She was quite pretty and very comforting. She told me I would be okay, no blood or compound fractures. Lots of sirens and a very uncomfortable ride to the Trauma center.

I am not sure how long I was laying in that street, because when I got to the trauma center, my wife and Pastor were already there or at least they were when I opened my eyes.

I believe the girl that was helping me called the I.C.E. (**In Case of Emergency**) number that was in my contacts on my phone. I wish I would have gotten her name. She was the Best.

I just plain hurt, everywhere. Five hours Later, The doctors come in and tell me they didn't think it was possible that they would be sending me home. Getting dressed with a lot of help, something barely touched my left arm and it hurt. More X-rays. Bone bruises, no breaks. Get dressed.

Outside, waiting for a ride, the world is getting dim. Out I went. Back to trauma again more testing. Nothing, get dressed. This time I made it home.

Mighty sore and bruised for a few days.

It turns out that it was my fault for operating a vehicle on a sidewalk. Five hours in the Trauma Center equals a bill of $26,000. ZERO deductible to the rescue.

Dr. Bill

Blogging with people about the Camino. I met Dr Bill from Florida. He was just leaving to do the Camino and so was a great help to me. I followed his blog all the way through. About half way through his trek I was starting to have some thoughts about his motive for trekking.

With a shock, I found out. The Newspapers in Florida carried the stories about his Son. His Son was a brilliant kid. He had two college degrees before he was 20. He was granted a fellowship to study for his Masters Degrees in Chinese and Arabic in China.

Just before leaving for China, Bill and his son Cullen were watching the movie,'The Way'. The same movie that got me. At the end of the movie, Cullen said he wanted to make the pilgrimage with his father as soon as he returned from China. It was agreed. After arriving in China, Cullen and several other students climbed to the top of their dorm to see the city at night. Cullen climbed even higher to get a better view. He slipped and fell six stories to his death.

Cullen's ashes made the pilgrimage in his fathers backpack. Dr. Bill is that kind of a man.

Corpus Christi to Dallas to Miami to Madrid. Of interest, I booked with American Airlines but when my tickets arrived, I noticed the flight from Miami to Madrid was on Iberia Airlines. I was nervous about that but it was too late to change.

What a surprise! The Iberia flight was on a brand new Airbus. Pretty Cool. The flight attendants were amazing. For the most part, they looked like Spanish Barbie Dolls. Tall and slender with long silky black hair. Lots of them. I think I counted at least 10 flight attendants. Naturally, mine was rather 'Frumpy' looking.

192

Lots of entertainment, 20 movies etc. My favorite was the avionics. Forward looking camera, Real time navigation maps, airspeed, all the neat stuff.

In contrast, the return flight from Madrid to Dallas was on an American Airlines flight. A VERY old plane and the flight attendants were my age.

The Air port in Madrid is BIG. We rode for a half mile on conveyor belts to retrieve luggage. It didn't make sense, it seemed like we rode the moving sidewalk for a long way in one direction then went down stairs and rode a conveyor belt a long way back in the direction we had come from. Sure enough, I looked out the windows and there was the underside of the plane we came in on. Oh Well, our luggage was there and after that many hours sitting, a walk was good.

The Barcelona Bullet

From the Airport, we went to Chamartin train station to catch a train to Ponferrada where our trek was to begin.

The Station was huge. Trains coming and going at an alarming rate. There were some sixteen sets of rails running through the station. It was all to simple. Just look at the electronic signage find your train and destination and go to the assigned gate. When the doors open, it's down the stairs to your train. Find your car #, get on and find your seat #. It's all on your ticket. Lots of people.

The train was super quiet. You could hear people talking at the other end of the car. Then I found that the trains ran on rubber tires. Clever and smooth.

As we climbed to 250+ kilometers an hour, I was amazed. Then I nearly peed myself. When you are traveling that fast and a train going that fast passes in the opposite direction, four feet from your face, it only takes a second. A very frightening second.

I would like to go back to Europe and tour using the rail system. It is that good, and it is cheap.

Trekking

We began our walk in Ponferrada Spain. Our original plan was to do the last 25% of the pilgrimage that was about 250 kilometers. If we were successful at that, we would transport back to do another segment. Anyone that completes the last 100km receives certification of completing the pilgrimage. Because of this, the last 100km of the pilgrimage has a lot more pilgrims than the first three fourths of the trek. You will meet a lot of people in the early stages, but many more in the latter.

Our first day was a short day. We had a late start because of a sleep-in. Jet Lag is tough. We did manage to trek nearly 20km and we were into the Wine country. Rolling hills, some rather steep.

Day two was a trip. We made it more than 30km. Part of that day was up and over a pretty serious mountain ridge. Not the Rocky mountains, but it was a strain.

A few days later, the first real trouble. After about 25km, my back started to tighten up. It got pretty bad. Over the next kilometers, I was leaning to the right at about a 30 degree list. I could not straighten up and it hurt. Had to stop numerous times.

We limped into a small town and found a Pharmacia. Every town has one. Dr. Bill from Florida had told me about a product called Voltarin (I think) that is a very powerful cream and it is amazing for aches and pains.

In the U.S. It is a prescription drug. In Spain, you can buy almost any drug over the counter.

It was wonderful. The next morning, I had Zero symptoms. The next couple of days were pain free and we did another 35km a day. The country and the people were fantastic. The grapes were being harvested so I tried some. Warning, tempranillo grapes are not intended for eating. Very tart.

Every town has a winery or has one nearby. At every meal, Tinto is offered free. Tinto and water, the same price. We found the local wines to be excellent. I never tasted one that I did not care for.

Then the pain came back with a 30 degree list to the left this time. 20 km into the trek, I had to lie down. 5 minutes, back underway. Not long, have to sit. 5 minutes underway. Down to 100 meters at a time.

Portomarin, Spain, another 4-5 days to Santiago. Decision time. We decided to abandon the trek, the pain was too much. We decided to take a bus the last 88km to Santiago and backtrack the Camino by car all the way to France.

I know the mistakes that were made. I should not have made such an aggressive schedule. If we had decided to just stop when tired, we would have made it. The Camino guide book is great if you are 20 years old. You should walk alone. If you have a 'partner', you will worry about them and not yourself. Set your own limits. Do not book round trip air fare. Leave return open. More expensive but then you can take as much time as you need.

Camino de Santiago

195

The Camino de Santiago has two types paths. Improved such as along a country road or a street through a village. The other paths are called natural paths that take you through farmlands, pastures and forests. These are the best paths. Every time we would see a section of natural paths coming, it was great. No cars, no trains, just the breeze in the trees and the birds. The perfect time to clear your head.

Albergues. A very interesting place to stay and sleep. For a small fee, you get a bunk bed and a shower. Very exclusive for you and 100 or so friends.

Things are different in Europe. The first albergue we stayed in was interesting. Setting up my bunk for the night, a college age girl comes walking by headed for a shower. She said 'hola' and continued on. What was unusual was she was wearing a bra and panties and carrying her towel and soap. Perfectly natural. Eventually, I just didn't pay attention.

More about 'The Way

People have been making this pilgrimage for more than twenty centuries. As you trek along, you will see markers where pilgrims have died trying to make it to Santiago.

Some areas of natural paths are worn down to as much as 6 feet below the surrounding area. Millions of footsteps will do that.

Estrella Galacia and Mahou beers are very tasty. Combine them with Tapas and you are good to go. MMMM good. Mahou I would say was the best. We did our best to help with the consumption of Beer and Tinto. As they say, when in Rome.......

Mahou Beer and Tapas. No way to explain how good they are. Better mention Tapas. Tapas are like free apps at a bar in the U.S. Only way better. Tapas can be a meal in itself. Some places are amazing. Just order a beer and you get a menu listing free Tapas. Several pages of them. You can get a hoagie type sandwich even shrimp on a skewer. All free.

Still hungry? Order another beer, more free Tapas. Full meal for about 4 Euros. Nice.

The local people made you feel welcome everywhere we went. The trekkers, lots of Canadians, Eh? Many college students. I found out that if a college student has on their resume that they have walked the Camino, it IS a big deal. We soon noted that 60+% of the trekkers were women. Many times they would be walking alone. It is that safe in Spain.

Auto Trekking

After arriving by Bus at Santiago, we saw the Cathedral of St James and it was very moving. We then toured Santiago for a few days. Then it was off to see Northern Spain by car.

We rented an Ibiza car. It is made by Volkswagen and has a little diesel engine. I was worried about that because we were going to be in the Pyrenees and other mountain areas. No need to worry, it had plenty of power and we got 46 miles per gallon of diesel. Yes, I converted kilometers to miles and liters of fuel to gallons.

I was quite nervous about driving in Spain. I had studied traffic rules for Spain on YouTube. It is far easier to drive in Spain than it is in the United States. Roads have three main categories, A=Super highways, B=main highways and N=country or rural. Simple.

We saw virtually no law enforcement, no accidents and No potholes. NONE. What?

I had loaded a free GPS navigator on my tablet for Spain and it was spot on perfect. A big help with traffic circles. The GPS girl would say , "At the traffic circle, take the third exit." She was never wrong. In Spain, there are very few 'Stop' signs. Most intersections are controlled with a traffic Circle. No stopping, just enter and get off at the proper exit. Cool.

Do you know what the letters are on a stop sign in Spain? If you guessed ALTO, you are wrong. Stop signs say STOP. ALTO in Spain means mountain top.

Our first stop was Finesterre known as the end of the Earth. This is where in Christopher Columbus' day was where if you sailed west to the horizon, you simply fell off the world. This is also kilometer marker zero for the Camino.

Muxia was next this is where the Bay of Biscay and the Atlantic Ocean Join. I took several hundred photos there of the surf and rocks.

I will not bore you with a travel log only to say that the Country of Spain is beautiful. I especially liked the Mountains. The Picos de Europas and the Pyrenees.

We saw Pamplona (Running of the Bulls) and many other notable sites.

While we were there, the Vuelta bicycle race was in action and we were nearly trapped by it once. The Vuelta is Spain's equivalent to the Tour de France. It is a very Big deal there. We drove one of the bicycle race routes and it was steep. I can't imagine how they race up a mountain that steep.

In the Roncal valley, I walked across Roman bridges that were built before the Birth of Christ.

Chapter 42
Cruz de Ferro

The Cruz de Ferro. It moved me in ways I thought were not possible. The Cruz de Ferro or Cross of Iron is located on a hilltop that is the highest point you would reach while walking the Camino de Santiago in Spain. It is known as a place of much significance.

While you walk the Camino, you carry a stone in your pocket and you place your life's burdens on that stone. When you reach the Cruz de Ferro, you leave your stone and your life's burdens behind. I was carrying three stones and a bracelet. The first stone I carried was for my friend Kyle and myself. That stone was small but it was very heavy with burdens. The second stone was for my son Michael. It had two girl's names on it that he had lost at childbirth. Those girls are at rest with my parents in the same grave site. The third stone was from Lake Ontario in New York that I carried for my friend Paul who had terminal cancer. The bracelet was for my Blog friend Dr. Bill from Florida. It was inscribed with the message, 'Camino With Cullen' in honor of his son that was tragically killed.

Being older, I am expected to be rock steady in all things. I will tell you that when I reached the Cruz de Ferro, I came unglued. I was there for some time before I could even speak. I finally got it together enough to say the words I had rehearsed a hundred times in my mind.

Leaving my Life's Burdens behind.

Every stone you see in this photo was carried by a Pilgrim from every corner of the World. Millions of stones from millions of trekkers. On the top at the base of the cross, you might still be able to find three stones and a bracelet placed there by me.

There was a presence there for me. Since then, I often have wondered was there really a spirit there or did I just want it to be? The answer is, it makes no difference. It moved me and that is what counts!

For me, the whole Camino de Santiago cleared one thing in my mind. All the formal religion that I have received boils down to just one thing, It's Me and God. If God is happy with me, I am happy with God.

It's that simple... Buen Camino my Friends

The Cross of St. James

Chapter 43

Madrid

I could probably write a whole book about Madrid. Lots of people and madness. That sounds worse than it was. If you are not driving, it is a cool place.

We were advised by the car rental people to avoid driving in Barcelona and Madrid. We elected to stay at Alcala de Henares that is about 45 kilometers northeast of Madrid. It was a great choice. We loved that place. A nice feature was that we stayed only one block from a train station. So it was to be that we would take a train to Madrid. We walked into the station to check schedules etc for the next day. Problem is, there is no human to talk to. Just a Big map of railroad tracks and the usual, 'You are here'. The Schedule is easy, there is a train every 10 minutes. A bit different from Amtrak's one train a week.

Tickets were easy, a bank of computerized ticket machines. Simple, touch the screen for the language you speak. All English now. What is your age? Senior. Where do yo want to go? Map says city center is Atocha station. Okay, how many tickets? Two. Please deposit 4 Euros, coin or credit card. Like magic, Two tickets appear. Simple. The only restriction is the tickets have to be used within two hours.

Early the next morning, we get our tickets. Now what? We head up the ramp to the Southbound track. We come to a series of gates. Put your ticket in a slot, the gate opens and your ticket reappears. Take your ticket and up the ramp. Within ten minutes, we are on a train headed into Madrid. No Conductor, nobody.

Watching a monitor on the train, a chime rings and the monitor says Atocha next. Cool. We get off the train and there are more gates. Put your ticket in and if it sees that you have paid to get there, the gates open and away you go.

Going up the ramp to the station main level, I could look across the sets of rails. There were at least a dozen trains loading or unloading. Busy!

The main level at Atocha station is a lot like a big airport in the U.S.

The City

The City itself was at first quite overwhelming. We were finishing up a month of simple country living. Very quiet and very slow paced. We step out of the Train station or more adequately, Estacion de Tren and we enter the world of horns, sirens, fast cars, motorcycles, bicycles and scooters. All are frantic.

Crossing a street is different. When you are clear to cross, there is a bird chirping noise and the posse crosses like a herd. Just outside the Estacion, there is a large traffic circle with a statue of King Carlos. I am trying to get a photo when I hear more sirens wailing. I see it across the traffic circle coming toward me. It's an ambulancia. It gets to the traffic

203

circle and turns LEFT into traffic. Yikes. He's taking the most direct route to the circle exit he wants. Oh please, don't put me in one of those. I guess it's an everyday thing. We were the only ones concerned with it.

A short walk and we are at the Botanical gardens and the Prada Museum that has many famous works of art. There are double decker buses everywhere. All loaded with touristas from around the world.

A street next to the gardens is for the Booksellers. Dozens of them in little shops maybe ten feet square. You could not go in any of them, they were so crammed with books.

Outside the Museum were the Artist wannabes. Some were really talented. Others were questionable.

Book Sellers

During our whole trip through Spain, we only met two grouchy people. We met number two at the Railroad museum. When we got there, we saw a row of those metal people barricade sections that didn't make much sense. They were not connected to anything. We saw on the outside of the building there was a flea market so we thought we would check it out.

Here comes this little Guarda lady walking fast., shaking her finger saying "NO ENTRY". She wasn't getting a lot of respect, she was like 5 feet nothing. I asked how do we get into the Museum. "NO, MUSEO CLOSED" . We watched for a while as she was chasing after everyone. I have some of it on video. We walked about 50 feet and it sure looked like the Museo was open. It was.

Later we just walked behind the lady that was trying to stop other people and went into the flea market.

Oh well, I could see why she would be grumpy.

The Railroad Museum was the former Train Station.

Chapter 44

It wasn't my Time

The summer of 2001 was spent in the Adirondack Mountains of Upstate New York. More specifically, Lake George. It was such a beautiful place. Being a Trout fisherman, it was disappointing. Acid rains had decimated the trout. I did get to fish the Ausable river that at one time was one of the premium streams in the United States. There were some big trout there, but do to fishing pressure, they were a tough catch.

We lived and worked at a large campground/RV park. It would have been great had it not been for the owner who was, let's say difficult. Each year, the park had virtually 100% turnover rate for employees. Not Good.

We still had a good time. We became good friends with Chuck and Sue from New Hampshire. We enjoyed listening to them talk with the letter 'R' missing from the English language.

We went to Saratoga for opening day of the horse racing. What a beautiful town. The actual racetrack is right in town. The city has grown around it. The whole facility was groomed to perfection.

Unique to Saratoga is that the Jockey dressing rooms are not under the grandstands. They are in a separate building. When it is race time, they come out and walk to the Paddock right through the race fans. Nothing roped off. They were like VERY colorful tourists.

One was walking right toward me. It was Gary Stevens. We made eye contact and he said, 'Hello'. I said, 'Good Luck'. A polite ,'Thank You'. I ran inside and bought a Win, Place, Show ticket on him and his horse. I wish I could say it was a winning move. I should have bought a Beer and a Hot Dog.

The atmosphere of Saratoga was well worth the lost wagering.

We loved New England and we started thinking about a summer in Maine. I put out a couple of inquiries without luck. As our time was winding down at Lake George we began planning our trip home to Texas. Suzanne wanted to see at least one show on Broadway. Planning begins to visit New York City.

The question comes up, what would I like to do there? Not being much the urban type, I said this trip is for you. The only thing I wanted to do in New York City was to have a very expensive Breakfast at the 'Windows of the World' restaurant high atop The World Trade Center. Agreed, we would do that the first morning and the rest of the time was hers for Broadway and shopping.

One week until we leave, I received an email from this man that owns an RV resort in Stonington Maine. Oh my gosh, this place sounds awesome. Stonington is one peninsula South from Bar Harbor. Talking it over, NYC is some distance South from Lake George. That means back North through Boston etc. Not fun.

It's decided, when we leave, it will be straight East across Vermont and New Hampshire then North to Stonington. Early morning September 10th, we head for Maine. Campground found. Wow, This is Beautiful.

The Owner says we will meet in the morning to discuss possible salaries etc. That's a first for campground workers.

September 11th, having a nice breakfast in the RV. Turn on the TV, oh my some airplane has hit the World Trade Center. Just as I am contemplating how some idiot pilot could be that far off course when.................Oh Lord, help those people! These planes were no accident......... The revelation hits! That was where I had planned on being. Was it Luck that I was in Maine? I am thinking more along the line of there is more for me to do in life. Thank you Lord.

Everyone knows where they were that day. Mine was rather chilling.

We met with the owner later and he described our duties for the next year. Suzanne would be front office and my job was to work with another man restoring his WWII fighter aircraft. Is that legal? I thought that work could only be done by FAA certified mechanics. He said no problem, he would be the only one flying it. I was not at all comfortable with this when he says the other guy is not certified either. We will think about it.

He invited us to stay free as many days as we would like. I'm still feeling ill about NYC. He invited us to a party that night because he has musician friends coming to Jam. Rather irreverent I would say. We passed on the party.

We elected to pass on these jobs. While we are here, LET'S EAT! We find our way to the town center and there we find a nice restaurant. It's not open yet, but there is a menu posted. Lobster dinner Forty dollars. What? Walk across the street and down a bank and you are in the Ocean. There must be two hundred lobster boats right there coming and going, it's lobster season. I can get a lobster dinner in Houston for that price.

Wandering around town, we go in a small 'Mom & Pop' grocery to pick up a couple of items. I mentioned to the man there that the Lobster dinner prices were crazy. He asked where we went? I pointed up the street. He looked around to see if anyone could hear and he said softly, 'Go down the hill to the Lobster docks. There is a cafe above the docks, that's where the locals eat.' No frills Lobster dinner. $9.95. Tea included. AWESOME! All neatly served steaming hot on Styrofoam. Now I understand, China plate rentals go for $30.05 each.

We pigged out on awesome lobster then went down to the docks and watched the lobsters being unloaded and sorted. I took some really cool pictures. It wasn't long and we were invited on the boat, well actually the Raven haired girl was invited, I just happened to be there. Photo ops with us holding huge Lobsters, one in each hand. Really cool.

Back upstairs we go. Two Lobster dinners to go please.

Stolen Truck

The next day, we relocated to Bar Harbor so we could visit Acadia National Park. Our RV spot was cool, walk out the back door and you were 10 feet from a quiet cove in the Ocean. The next morning, I woke up and went outside to find the Ocean was about a mile away. Guys out there on the mud flats crawling around digging up giant worms. They say they get 50 cents apiece for the worms.

Off to Acadia National Park. Bar Harbor and the Park were being frequented by Classic Cars. Rolls Royces, Bentleys and many I didn't recognize. The park was spectacular to say the least.

At one point we stopped for Photo ops at an overlook. Amazing surf crashing the rocks. The parking was easy, we were past the tourist season now so visitors were few. The parking area was quite long, maybe 100 yards or more and had several rows for parking. There were very few cars there. Most were of the Classic variety. I parallel parked right by the observation area and we hopped out to 'Observe'.

A short time later, we decided to move along. Much to our dismay, we had no means of transportation. My pride and joy was gone. Just plain GONE. How can this happen? Full blown PANIC! How could someone steal my truck when I was only 50 feet away? Then I see it. It's easily 200 yards away. It rolled all the way down through the parking area, out onto the Park road for another hundred yards then on the far side of the road into a shallow ditch and stopped rolling. Right through about a million dollars worth of cars and down the highway without hitting anything. Amazingly, I don't think anyone noticed there was no driver. Jesus had taken the wheel.

Close examination revealed someone did not leave the truck in gear or used the emergency brake. I never said a word to her about that. She should have known better.

Chapter 45

Women

Women naturally, were a major factor in my life. Below are those that have had the most affect on my life from the first to last. At this point, Imagine Willie Nelson singing "To all the girls I've Loved before".

My Mom. She was born in Lancashire England and emigrated to the United States when she was only four. Mom was the True North of our family. Always kept us on the right heading. She was far to easy on her son. She should have been tougher on me because I did things that were not good. I should weigh a ton, because she surely knew how to cook. She tried in vain to teach me, but I never could get the feeling for a fist full of this and a pinch or two of that. When I was in High School, she always told me I should take a typing class. What? You gotta be kidding. So here I am at this very moment pecking away at this keyboard with a couple of fingers. As always, you were right Mom.

When Mom made up her mind, she knew what she wanted. For example, Mom and Dad were engaged over ten years while my Dad was off to Florida to play Semi Pro Baseball. It was a good thing for me that she stuck it out.

Love you Mom.

My sister Margaret (Peggy)

My sister Margaret was the smart one, High School valedictorian. All the good stuff.

She was a great help to me when I was **Coming of Age**. She could talk to me about anything. I was never confident when I was around other girls. My sister coached me through some scary times when I was interested in some particular girl. I guess she let me see behind the curtain, so to speak, about how girls think.

She would often drive my friends and I to the movies or high school sports. That made her pretty cool with my friends.

My sister died when she was 38. It just didn't seem fair. Leukemia is not fair. Two years before she died, the family was summoned to be with her at her death bed when for some reason, she went into remission. Later, she told me about her 'Near Death' experience. The Bright light, the

Curtain, the Angles, all of it. That conversation has remained with me all through my life. For her remaining two years, she gave many talks to religious groups and to those suffering with terminal illnesses. She was that kind of woman.

When she died, my dad got terribly depressed until I moved them to Texas and got my dad fishing again. Every year on my sister's birthday, meant a week or so of depression for my dad.

Love you Sis.

Judy, my first real girl friend. I was wild about her. We were an item for four years. Things went wrong. I had too many Loves. She is leaning on one of them. I just didn't know how to treat a woman. It's easy to blame the other half, but it just was not my time.

Judy, the cheerleader. I often wonder if she still has my High School sweater seen here. It was a big deal to me. I would like to have it back please.

It's okay, you gave me memories that will last forever.

I met Toni at the Pizza Villa in Warrensburg Missouri. She was a student at Southwest Missouri State. I was a Rocket Scientist for the U.S. Air Force. Her friends talked her into going that night and my friends drug me along.

The beer was cold, the music was good and I spotted her. Love at first sight? She was a hottie for sure. Dance with me? Okay. She was a tad sarcastic at first but it was Bud and Toni from that night on.

Happy ever after was not to be. I blamed her for a long time before I realized I had no idea of how to be a good husband. For that I am sorry.....

She presented me with the best gifts ever, Jeffrey and Michael.

After we split, we got along better than we did when we were married. When the boys reached Junior high, she let them come and live with me. I am forever thankful for that.

Found this Hottie in the Yellowstone Canyon
Asked her to Hike with me. She said YES
Still Hiking with me all over the World !

Suzanne

This Raven haired Italian beauty came into my life while we were both employed by duPont at LaPorte Texas. She was actually my typist. No Computers then. She was a real beauty. Long black silky hair. All the good stuff.

We started dating at the end of 1984 and we still go on dates as of this writing. Life is Good.

We have traveled a lot. 46 of the 48 states plus Alaska, several of the Provinces of Canada and Europe. I think I have learned a lot about relationships and I try very hard to be a good husband.

Britt

My stepdaughter Britt came into my life as a 'Package' deal with Suzanne. It was great until she found she was going to have to relocate with Mom. She hated me for that.

It was a long slow process, but we finally worked it out. Today, she is the daughter I always wanted.

There you have it, The women that made me who I am.

I Loved them all !

Coming of Age and More

Epilogue

The stories and tales you have read are as true and as factual as my memory would permit. You have probably noticed that I have omitted the last names of characters in this book. This was done to insure I would not intentionally offend anyone.

If you were mentioned in this book, I tried to send each of you the chapter you were mentioned in. Thus giving you a chance to defend yourself. I am thankful to all that responded with their support and also for jogging my memory about missing details and forgotten events.

Some time ago, my original outline for this memoir became overloaded with things to write about. I believe I could do a sequel with no problem.

I wish I would not have thrown away my original Outline. It was covered with arrows, doodles, various notes, scratch outs etc. My original outline would have made no sense to anyone but me. It was more like a treasure map in Cryptic Code.

If I have departed before you read this and wonder where I have gone,,,,,,,,,,,,,

Read **John 5:24.**

It is right there!

You see,

I do Believe !

218

219

Credits

My most sincere thanks to those that encouraged me, motivated me, assisted me, provided lost memories and most importantly inspired me to do this.

Jim Austin
Paul Austin
Clyde Burmaster
Tom Kersten
Dr. William Klein
Jeffrey Schultz
Michael Schultz
Suzanne Schultz
Britt Stone
Dave & Sandy Stott
Iva Streeter

It was a great ride, **Coming of Age.**

Looking back on my life, If I could change one thing, what would it be? I had to think about this for a while.

I think it would be that I would like everyone from my past to know how deeply I cared for them. Love You!

Bud

43847167R00132

Made in the USA
San Bernardino, CA
30 December 2016